JOHN LEA

077-30-0109

2-

MOGADISHU!

Rangers "fast-roping" from a Blackhawk helicopter.

MOGADISHU!

Heroism and Tragedy

Kent DeLong and Steven Tuckey

Foreword by Ross Perot

Westport, Connecticut
London

Library of Congress Cataloging-in-Publication Data

DeLong, Kent.
    Mogadishu! : heroism and tragedy / Kent DeLong and Steven Tuckey ;
    foreword by Ross Perot.
        p. cm.
    ISBN 0–275–94925–7
        1. Operation Restore Hope, 1992-1993. 2. Somalia—History—1991–
    I. Tuckey, Steven. II. Title.
    DT407.D45 1994
    967.7305—dc20   94–31744

British Library Cataloguing in Publication Data is available.

Library of Congress Catalog Card Number: 94–31744
ISBN: 0–275–94925–7

First published in 1994

Praeger Publishers, 88 Post Road West, Westport, CT 06881
An imprint of Greenwood Publishing Group, Inc.

Printed in the United States of America

∞™

The paper used in this book complies with the
Permanent Paper Standard issued by the National
Information Standards Organization (Z39.48–1984).

10 9 8 7 6 5 4 3 2 1

This book is dedicated to the following special people:

Jeanne, Lindsay, Camden, and Everett DeLong

Dorothy Tuckey and to the memory of Thomas Tuckey

To the memory of Winona Millett

To the families who gave us their sons, their brothers, and their fathers:

The Cavaco Family
The Smith Family
The Kowalewski Family
The Briley Family
The Joyce Family
The Houston Family
The Wolcott Family
The Field Family
The Gordon Family
The Cleveland Family
The Frank Family
The Shughart Family
The Busch Family
The Pilla Family
The Ruiz Family
The Fillmore Family
The James Martin Family
The Timothy Martin Family

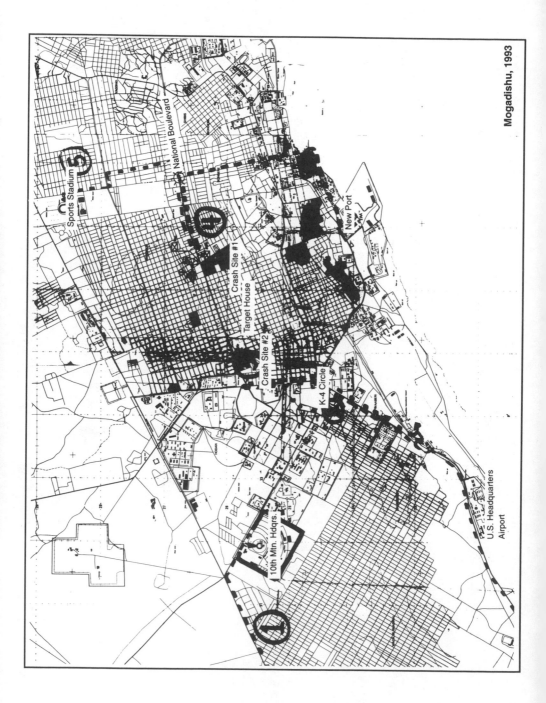

Mogadishu, 1993

Contents

Foreword by Ross Perot   ix

Chronology of Events   xi

Major Participants   xiii

Introduction   xvii

Chapter 1   1

Chapter 2   7

Chapter 3   13

Chapter 4   21

Chapter 5   27

Chapter 6   31

Chapter 7   39

Chapter 8   45

Chapter 9   53

Chapter 10   61

Chapter 11   67

Chapter 12   75

Chapter 13   81

Chapter 14   89
Chapter 15   93
Chapter 16   99
Epilogue   101
Glossary   103
Index   105

Photo essay follows page 44.

Foreword

Every American should read this book in order to gain a clear insight about military combat and war.

It is important for every American to understand that—

• Peace-keeping missions can suddenly turn into all-out war, even if only for a short period of time.

• Our troops, our sons and daughters, can get killed and wounded, just as if they were involved in a large-scale war.

• Death is just as final in Mogadishu as it was in World War II.

• The sacrifices demanded of families are just as intense. Children must grow up without a parent. The surviving parent must bear the pain of losing a loved one, and assume the responsibility of rearing the children alone.

Finally,

• These missions demand the same level of patriotism and heroism as Americans showed on the beaches of Normandy and Iwo Jima, even though we tend to think of them as tiny wars.

• Read about these magnificent men who risked and gave their lives in broad daylight to save their comrades. They are classic examples that, "Greater love hath no man than he lay down his life for a friend."

Television reporting of war has turned it into a spectator event that can be confused with athletic contests. Peace-keeping missions, when they become war, exact a terrible price.

When our nation sends our sons and daughters into combat, we must have a clearly defined mission. The mission must be so important that you or I would send our own sons and daughters to fight and die for it.

Our military troops love this country and are willing to fight and die for it. We have an enormous obligation not to take advantage of their idealism and patriotism.

The relevant question to ask before sending these men and women into combat is, would you and I be willing to die for this cause?

Read this book carefully. Never forget its contents as you watch the TV docu-dramas of smart bombs going down air shafts, where war is presented in a sterile, sanitized environment. Remember, war is fighting and dying.

This book honors our heroes.

Chronology of Events

October 3, 1993

1:00 P.M.	Joint Operations Command Center briefing where intelligence was bared indicating top Farid Aidid lieutenants were ready for the picking.
2:15 P.M.	Task Force Ranger places section of Mogadishu off limits; first indication to various U.S. units throughout city that operation might occur.
3:30 P.M.	Lead pilot gets "Irene" code word; mission begins.
3:37 P.M.	Task Force Ranger headquarters issues REDCON ONE alert keeping men on 30-minute "string."
3:50 P.M.	Ground convoy arrives in position waiting for signal to load prisoners.
Around 4:00 P.M.	Insertion complete with assault forces and blockers on the outside doing their job; enemy fire starting to increase.
4:10 P.M.	First notification of Cliff Wolcott's downed helicopter.
4:20 P.M.	Michael Durant's helicopter is shot down about a mile to the south of first crash site.
4:30 P.M.	Ground convoy attempts to reach Wolcott crash site but runs into fierce Somali resistance.
	10th Mountain Quick Reaction Force summoned to airport.
4:35 P.M.	Snipers Shughart and Gordon dropped off at Durant crash site to help fend off armed crowds.
5:00 P.M.	Ground convoy decides to forsake rescue mission after taking too many injuries and returns to airfield.

5:15 P.M.	Hastily assembled Ranger rescue team takes off for Wolcott crash site and encounters furious resistance.
5:24 P.M.	QRF arrives at airport for intense rescue planning.
6:18 P.M.	Ground convoy arrives at airfield.
6:30 P.M.	QRF force takes off in combat column for rescue effort at Durant crash site.
7:00 P.M.	QRF column is forced to turn back after encountering fierce Somali firepower.
7:20 P.M.	Ranger company at Wolcott crash site establishes defense perimeter to wait for rescue force.
8:30 P.M.	Planning just about complete at airport for multinational rescue force that includes QRF soldiers aided by Malaysian and Pakistani armored vehicles and personnel.
10:40 P.M.	Relief column including about 300 soldiers from three nations ready to pull out.
11:30 P.M.	Relief column pulls out.
Midnight	Two APCs with rescue troops heading for northern (Wolcott) crash site turn south instead and end up stranded after being hit by Somali RPG attack.
1:50 A.M.	QRF relief column arrives at Wolcott crash site.
3:00 A.M.	Stranded rescuers picked up by Malaysian APCs from troops at southern (Durant) crash site.
5:20 A.M.	QRF and Rangers extract bodies from Wolcott crash site and prepare to move back to the airport.
5:45 A.M.	Convoy arrives back at sports stadium.

Major Participants

Jones, Chief Warrant Officer Randy—Task Force Ranger Pilot of his "little bird" attack helicopter Barber 51.

Matthews, Lieutenant Colonel Tom—Air Mission Commander from the 160th Special Aviation Regiment.

Garrison, Major General William—Task Force Ranger commander.

Aidid, General Mohammed Farid—Somalian warlord and target of the United Nations manhunt, in general, and October 3 mission in specific.

Cugno, Major Ron—STAR wing assault commander flying MH-6 "little bird" helicopter.

Wade, CW3 Hal—Co-pilot and wing leader for Jones in "little bird" attack helicopter.

Kulsrud, Chief Warrant Officer Larry—Pilot of "Little Bird" attack helicopter Barber 52.

Wolcott, Cliff—75th Ranger and Blackhawk Super 61 pilot shot down on October 3 after inserting Delta Force troops at target site.

Goffena, Michael—75th Ranger and Blackhawk Super 62 pilot and part of the insertion team.

Perino, Lieutenant Larry—3rd Ranger Battalion, B Company platoon and mission chalk position leader.

Steele, Captain Mike—3rd Ranger Battalion and B Company commander.

Durant, Michael—160th Regiment Blackhawk helicopter Super 64 pilot shot down and held captive by Somalis for 10 days.

DiTomasso, Lieutenant Tom—3rd Ranger Battalion B Company platoon and mission chalk position leader.

Cleveland, Sergeant Bill—Durant's Super 64 crew chief.

Fields, Sergeant Tommie—Durant's Super 64 crew chief.

Eversman, NCO Sergeant Matthew—Ranger platoon leader inserted at target building.

Elliott, Sergeant Charles—Ranger at target building.

Heard, Private First Class Brian—Ranger at target building who was ordered to shoot armed, threatening Somalis.

Briley, Donovan—Wolcott's co-pilot who died in the downing of his Super 61 Blackhawk.

Jollota, Dan—160th Regiment and pilot of the Combat Search and Rescue helicopter who first was at Wolcott's crash site.

Lamb, Sergeant First Class Al—CSAR insertion team lead in Jollota's chopper.

Belda, Sergeant Mark—Weapons team member in CSAR chopper.

Maier, Chief Warrant Officer Karl—Pilot of STAR 41 "little bird" MH-6 gunship that aided Wolcott rescue effort.

Jones, Chief Warrant Officer Keith—Maier's co-pilot who aided in Wolcott rescue effort.

Ward, Hal—Crew member of the "little bird" gunship.

Belman, Sergeant John—CSAR soldier in Jollota's craft.

Stebbins, Specialist John—CSAR soldier in Jollota's chopper sent to aid rescue efforts at downed Wolcott helicopter site.

McKnight, Lieutenant Colonel Danny—3rd Battalion, 75th Ranger regiment— leader of the truck convoy that was to remove captives from the target building, but was diverted to failed rescue attempt at Wolcott crash site.

Powell, Sergeant Bill—75th Ranger Regiment in charge of McKnight ground convoy fire support team.

Carlson, Private First Class Tory—Part of McKnight ground convoy.

Cavaco, Corporal James—Mark 19 gunner in McKnight ground convoy shot and killed.

Pringle, Sergeant Michael—Ground convoy machine gunner.

Galleher, Sergeant Bob—Ground convoy driver.

Joyce, Corporal James J.—Killed in McKnight ground convoy rescue attempt.

Weaver, Sergeant Aaron—Ground convoy driver.

Williamson, Sergeant Aaron—Ranger in a blocking position at the target house who was shot when he was on a mission to rescue other soldiers in danger at the Wolcott crash site.

Smith, Corporal James—Ranger fatally shot trying to aid at Wolcott crash site.

Blackburn, Sergeant Todd—Chalk Four Ranger who was injured in original insertion.

Ruiz, Sergeant Lorenzo—Killed in the ground convoy.

Kowaleski, Private First Class Richard—Ranger killed in the ground convoy.

Warner, Sergeant Mark—Ranger trying to assist the ground convoy.

Fillmore, Sergeant First Class Earl—Ranger killed in attempt to reach Wolcott crash site.

Boorn, Sergeant Kenneth—Ranger shot in first attempt to reach Wolcott crash site.

Rodriguez, Specialist Carlos—Ranger shot in first attempt to reach Wolcott crash site.

Goodale, Sergeant Mike—Ranger fire control officer taking part in first attempt to reach Wolcott crash site.

Frank, Ray—Slain co-pilot in Durant's doomed Super 64 Blackhawk.

Hall, Sergeant Mason—Door gunner in Goffena Super 62 Blackhawk.

Field, Tommie—Slain crew chief in Durant's doomed Super 64 Blackhawk.

Gordon, Master Sergeant Gary—Delta Force sniper killed in attempt to rescue Durant. Later awarded Medal of Honor.

Shughart, Sergeant First Class Randy—Delta Force sniper killed in attempt to rescue Durant. Later awarded Medal of Honor.

Shannon, Crew Chief Paul—Crew chief in Goffena's Blackhawk Super 62.

Yacone, Captain Jim—Goffena's co-pilot.

Halling, Bradley—Sniper in Goffena's Super 62 Blackhawk.

David, Lieutenant Colonel William—Commander of 10th Mountain Quick Reaction Force.

Flaherty, Lieutenant Michael—QRF medic.

Casper, Colonel Lawrence—10th Mountain Aviation Brigade commander.

Harold, Lieutenant Colonel Bill—Delta Force commander.

Gile, Brigadier General Greg—10th Mountain Division commander.

Whetstone, Captain Mike—10th Mountain QRF Charlie Company commander.

Montgomery, Major General—10th Mountain commander who led the multinational effort to rescue trapped Rangers at the two helicopter crash sites.

Carroll, Sergeant—Wounded QRF soldier rescued by Sergeant Doody in first ill-fated rescue attempt.

Pamer, Private First Class Eugene—QRF soldier shot in first ill-fated rescue attempt; Silver Star recipient.

Knight, Sergeant Richard—QRF soldier in first ill-fated rescue attempt.

Durant, Lorrie—Wife of Michael Durant who kept home fires burning waiting for his return from captivity.

Gore, Lieutenant Colonel Robert Lee—Commander of 10th Mountain "Raven" attack helicopter company.

Neely, Jim—Pilot in "Raven" company.

Nixon, Major Craig—Liaison from Task Force Ranger to QRF.

Aspin, Les—Secretary of Defense until January of 1994.

Powell, General Colin—Chairman of Joint Chiefs of Staff through 1993.

Doody, First Sergeant Gary—Charlie Company soldier who received numerous awards for valor under fire.

Hollis, Lieutenant Mark—QRF Alpha Company platoon leader stranded in a wrong-way convoy.

Meyerowich, Captain Drew—QRF Alpha Company commander sent to Wolcott crash site rescue effort.

Moores, Lieutenant Larry—Ranger who helped lead a hastily assembled convoy to rescue survivors at Wolcott crash site.

Warner, Sergeant Mark—Ranger who helped lead a hastily assembled convoy to rescue survivors at Wolcott crash site.

Mita, First Sergeant David—10th Mountain Alpha Company NCO sent to rescue Rangers at Wolcott crash site.

Martin, Private First Class James—10th Mountain soldier who died on way to Wolcott crash site rescue.

Howard, Lieutenant Colonel Bill—Special Forces officer who accompanied QRF rescue effort to Wolcott crash site.

Liles, Sergeant First Class John—Senior medic for 160th Aviation Regiment.

Adams, Dr. Bruce—160th Regiment surgeon key to hospital operations after the mission.

Borton, Tommie—Adams's medic assistant.

March, Dr. Bruce—Special Forces surgeon who helped set up casualty collection point near the airport's tarmac.

Uhorachak, Major John—Army orthopedic surgeon helping to staff field hospital that day.

Martin, Master Sergeant Tim "Grizz"—Special Forces soldier killed in action.

Simpson, Staff Sergeant Michael—Forward Area Rearming and Refueling Point chief armament technician.

Harrison, Chuck—Pilot.

Seipel, Specialist John—QRF soldier shot but not seriously injured when Crash Site One rescue convoy pulled out Monday morning.

DeJesus, Specialist Melvin—Ranger who was stranded at Wolcott crash site.

Houston, Sergeant Cornell—QRF soldier who was killed in action.

Introduction

Few things grab American interest more than pictures of starving children. And so, in the early 1990s when we were shown the television pictures of the terrible famine in the Horn of Africa, we wanted action. We didn't have much of an idea of what caused this famine or even where these children were. In fact, most of us had never spent much time thinking about this area of the world. We generally knew nothing about the civil war in Somalia, which in recent years had replaced former dictator Siad Barré with a confusing array of subclans intent on destroying each other. It really didn't matter much to us that the current leaders of Somalia were more interested in their own power than the well-being of their fellow citizens.

By December 1992 American celebrities, accompanied by increasingly grim television pictures of starvation and suffering, had made it clear that the gargantuan might of the U.S. military was needed. And President George Bush, in the waning days of his defeated administration, would have had it no other way.

The landing of U.S. Marines on the beaches of Mogadishu was dramatic, but overdone. The American soldiers weren't met on the beaches by enemy soldiers, or even by Somalis. They were met by other Americans: photographers and newspeople who were busy interviewing the troops to get the story.

The Somali clansmen weren't quite sure what to make of this. And there was no question that the Americans had no idea what was ahead for them. What the American troops soon learned was that the Somalis in power were in no mood to give up anything in the interests of feeding starving people. In fact, this mission was not going to be the simple one of distributing food and supplies. It was going to be much more political, much more military, and much more complex.

When clan leader General Mohammed Farid Aidid burst into the world scene so brilliantly with a $25,000 price tag on his head in June 1993, he became the appointed enemy that U.N. Chief Boutros Boutros-Ghali wanted. Aidid had been responsible for massacres of U.N. peacekeeping troops and was clearly the bad guy we so desperately needed. On the other hand, this clan leader was a key piece in the puzzle of nation-building, which had apparently also become a goal of American involvement in Somalia.

Unfortunately, while one American hand was trying to disarm and destroy Aidid, another hand was evidently trying to include him in the political process. This confusion went to the highest levels. This was seen best in August 1993 when Secretary of State Les Aspin denied the requests of his field commanders and refused to give his men sufficient armored equipment to conduct their missions. Evidently Aspin was afraid these requests for Bradley fighting vehicles and more efficient air support would be seen as military posturing while a political solution was being pursued.

No one told the young American soldiers about the political solution. They were there as fighting men and fight they would.

The streets of Mogadishu are not the same as the deserts of Kuwait. The difference between the safety of the secured Mogadishu airport and the urban enemy killing fields may have been separated by only a few blocks, but to soldiers pinned down with little help, it may just as well have been a hundred miles.

When the fighting began in the afternoon of October 3, 1993, the American troops knew they were in for the battle of their lives. When every civilian is a potential enemy, no fighting is easy. When every battleground is filled with hostile civilians—people you thought you were there to help—the fighting becomes not only difficult, it becomes nearly impossible.

Chapter 1

"Barber Five One, this is Atom Five One, Irene. Irene."

Chief Warrant Officer Randy Jones was sitting on the runway in his "little bird" attack helicopter, Barber 51. His was the lead aircraft of the sixteen helicopter Task Force Ranger fleet, all of whom were waiting on the runway behind him.

Lieutenant Colonel Tom Matthews was plugged into the special electronic communications system of his top-secret UH-60 Blackhawk helicopter near the rear of the fleet. His "Command and Control" bird had just received the go-ahead signal from Task Force Ranger commander Major General William Garrison in the Tactical Operations Center. The "Irene" code was passed on to Randy Jones in the lead attack aircraft. It was time to proceed. The mission was on.

The pilots were anxious and ready to get started. It was 3:30 P.M. on Sunday, October 3, 1993. An eventful day awaited them.

Sixteen helicopters from the supersecret 160th Special Aviation Regiment spun their blades, preparing to follow Jones into battle. The choppers were carrying nearly one hundred of the U.S. military's most elite soldiers: the men of Delta Force and the U.S. Army Rangers.

The Task Force objective was to capture the top lieutenants of General Mohammed Aidid, whose men had been regularly ambushing and killing soldiers from the U.N. peacekeeping force in Somalia. Intelligence had just been received that at least two of Aidid's close aides, men important enough to be on the Task Force Ranger "top ten hit-list," were meeting nearby.

"Mog tower, Barber Five One, element departure Two Three." Jones let the control tower know they were leaving on the southwest runway. The awesome power of sixteen Special Forces helicopters shook the ground.

The fleet used its normal takeoff sequence, following the leader with three-second intervals. The first group of aircraft flew slowly for the first three miles to allow the fleet pattern to form. Some of the aircraft were heavily loaded with as many as sixteen assault troops: the two lead little bird gunships carried a full load of rockets.

The first checkpoint north of the city came into view. The radios crackled, "Barber Five One, this is Atom Five One. Lucy. Lucy."

Lucy was the code word the fleet had been waiting for, Lucy was the signal to attack. All actions of the fleet were now event-driven. There were no more time schedules. Major Ron Cugno, the STAR wing assault commander flying an MH-6 little bird helicopter in the middle of the fleet, told his co-pilot, "It's rock 'n' roll time."

The men from the 160th were experienced veterans. This certainly wasn't the first time they had received orders to attack. Formed in 1980 as a response to the failed attempt in the desert raid to rescue hostages from Iran, the men of the 160th from Fort Campbell, Kentucky, had become the "wheels" and the fire support for U.S. Special Forces troops. Wherever any Special Forces operation needs to go, the "Night Stalkers" of the 160th takes them there. After insertion, the 160th supports them with surgical machine-gun fire. There is no question that the 160th represents the "best of the best" in military aviation.

The 160th pilots had been the lead elements during the invasion of Grenada and Panama. Other past missions had them searching Iranian waters for patrol boats that attacked oil tankers. One mission had them sinking Iranian patrol boats laying mines in the Persian Gulf. During Desert Storm, these men flew brazenly throughout the Iraqi countryside, carrying Green Berets searching for Scud Missile launch sites.

Because all missions of the 160th are classified and nearly all occur at night in enemy territory, most of the Night Stalker activities remain unknown outside of Special Operations. Their regiment motto is "death waits in the dark," but their actions are rarely talked about. In fact, until recently, the Pentagon did not admit the existence of this elite force of pilots.

For security reasons, the unit's classified little bird attack helicopters aren't flown during daylight unless absolutely necessary.

But on this operation, the entire fleet was in the air—under a bright sun—as Randy Jones's lead Barber 51 little bird approached the target house. The rest of the fleet sped up and waited for the "bump." The so-called "bump" occurs when Jones's lead aircraft initiates the fleet's attack by gaining altitude and then diving at a nearly vertical angle into the target.

The focus of the attack was a house in the center of Aidid's "Black Sea" stronghold in Mogadishu. The U.N. forces had never secured this area and had rarely risked their lives venturing into the place. The stronghold was just to the east of the Bakara gun market, a bazaar where anyone could buy an AK-47 assault rifle for $150. This heavily populated, hostile area was only two miles from U.N. military headquarters—an area considered by many to be "the most dangerous neighborhood in Africa."

Earlier in the afternoon, a member of the Abgal clan, the major rival to Aidid's Habar-Gedir subclan, had followed a car carrying some of Aidid's lieutenants to this house. These lieutenants had been attending the weekly Sunday afternoon anti-U.N. and anti-U.S. rally at the sports stadium. They had come to this house for a meeting with other subclan leaders, and possibly Aidid himself.

The Abgal clan member had given a signal to a Navy P-3 Orion spy plane circling high overhead in the sky of Mogadishu. The agent opened the hood of his car and then walked around it twice. His gesture was the signal that told the commanders in the Task Force Ranger Tactical Operations Command (TOC) headquarters that the "targets" were in the house.

The Task Force Ranger commanders knew it was time to activate the world's most highly trained and effective military "extraction unit." The time had come to take the "PC," or human "precious cargo."

As pilot Randy Jones in Barber 51 approached the target area, there were many decisions to be made. His co-pilot and wing leader, CW3 Hal Wade, monitored the thermoscanners for people outside the building. He was relieved to see neither posted guards nor civilians wandering around in the area.

A lucky break.

The Olympic Hotel and the target house were coming in view as Jones and his little bird wingman, Chief Warrent Officer Larry Kulsrud in Barber 52, were now speeding south. They had just passed over the burned-out cigarette factory, which until a month ago had been the base of operations for Aidid.

The lead pilots still couldn't see the "signal car" because it was on the south side of the house and the fleet had looped around and were entering from the north. They could see that the target house had antennas on it, a fact that made it stand out in the dense slums of Mogadishu.

Three cars were outside the target house. These were what the Task Force members called "Klingon Cruisers" named after the Star Trek "bad guy" spaceships. The cruisers (actually Toyota Landcruisers with bars on the back) were a common form of transportation for residents in Mogadishu. These vehicles got the name Klingon Cruisers because there were usually "Twenty-two people clinging on" to the bars on back wherever they went.

Jones's lead aircraft began increasing altitude about four hundred feet in preparation of the "bump," a nearly vertical dive directly into the target. The fleet behind watched closely to see if Barber 51 and 52 would need to fire their weapons. The other pilots were relieved when they saw the lead aircraft bump down without firing.

The entire fleet prepared for battle and accelerated as it went into an offensive flight profile. There was maximum visibility for the pilots and so far everything was going according to plan.

Four STAR aircraft carrying three Special Forces "customers" each, along with two powerful Blackhawk helicopters, each carrying twelve more, began hovering around the target building. The pilots called their Special Forces passengers "customers." The "customers" were Delta Force Green Berets from Fort Bragg, North Carolina, Air Force "P.J.s" and Navy SEALS, and the elite U.S. Army Rangers from Fort Benning, Georgia.

These insertion forces quickly "fast-roped" out the sides of their aircraft to the ground. The Task Force Ranger soldiers were experts at this maneuver. Ropes were dropped over the sides of the helicopters and the men rapidly slid to the ground with nothing protecting them except leather gloves.

One of the STAR aircraft landed directly on top of the target building and discharged Special Forces troops onto the roof, while other helicopters ringed the building with a torrent of troop delivery activity. Delta Force quickly entered the luckless structure to begin a well-rehearsed and deadly building security operation.

Four more Blackhawk helicopters arrived with members of the 75th Rangers from Fort Benning, Georgia. Their mission was to place troops in blocking positions on the streets and intersections outside the building. A model of forceful and well-rehearsed choreography, these soldiers quickly secured the area to keep anyone from entering or leaving.

Pilot Jones, along with his wingman flying over the operation, observed everything as they began a low orbit of the area. They could see a "honeywagon shit truck" (or septic tank truck) sitting at one of the planned blocking intersections and they reported it.

Immediately, all five of Jones's radios began to buzz.

Reports about Somalis trying to get into the area filled the radio waves. Vehicles began moving everywhere. Spot reports about sporadic ground fire began. Jones and his co-pilot Wade watched a gunfight start on the ground between some of the inserted Rangers and Somali gunmen.

By now there was a dense blanket of dust and dirt kicked up by the insertion helicopters around the building. Jones could see that the troop insertion had been accomplished and both the assault forces and the blocking forces were doing their work.

The attack little birds—Barber 51 and 52—went into their "high cap." This was a three hundred-foot circling orbit around and above the target building. Two other assault Blackhawks, Super 61 and 62 piloted by Cliff Wolcott and Michael Goffena, had just inserted Delta Force and were now in a 150-foot "low cap" orbit directly over the building.

The enemy fire started to increase.

The bullets were coming from windows, doorways, and rooftops. There were no tracers, so it was difficult for the pilots to tell exactly where the fire was coming from. They could hear the occasional ping of a bullet hitting the side of their aircraft and even their rotor blades.

However, when the rocket-propelled grenade (RPG) fire began, the mission changed. The character of this afternoon had become more serious. Everyone knew the ground mission needed to be completed soon, so the helicopters could get out of there.

An extraction ground force waited a half mile away for the orders to go in and take the ground soldiers and any prisoners away. But it wasn't quite time yet.

Randy Jones began seeing air bursts from fired RPGs exploding at preset altitudes, usually around 1,500 feet. So far, no one had been hit; but Jones had seen a lot of combat (beginning in Vietnam almost twenty-five years before) and he wasn't sure how much longer this would stay true. Things were heating up and it was clearly only a matter of time before something happened.

A true Southern boy by birth and spirit, Randy Jones was born in Westpoint, Mississippi, in 1949. He joined the army when he was twenty and a year later was flying Cobra gunships in Vietnam. During his year there, he logged 850 combat hours and received 34 air medals flying 6 days a week. He saw more than his share of buddies killed.

In 1980, he became one of the original pilots for the 158th, which later became the 160th Special Aviation Regiment. He saw action in the Persian Gulf protecting oil tankers from Iranians and, later in Panama, led a helicopter assault on the Rio Hato Air Force Base during Operation Just Cause. During Operation Desert Shield, he chased around the Iraqi countryside transporting Special Forces ground troops well before the ground invasion began.

There weren't too many active helicopter pilots who had seen the level of combat that Jones had. Now balding with a little age, but still compact and handsome with an easy, open personality, he thought that just maybe he was getting a little too old for this stuff.

"Six One hit. Six One hit. Blackhawk going down."

Cliff Wolcott's terrified words filled the airways and every pilot's intensity increased another notch. Everyone saw it.

Wolcott's Super 61 Blackhawk was flying the low cap over the target building. The doomed aircraft had just turned sideways to allow the side gunner a clearer shot at an RPG launch site. Thus, the Blackhawk presented a broadside target for the Somali ground gunner who immediately took full advantage of the opportunity. With a lucky shot, the gunner put a rocket-propelled grenade right into Wolcott's main rotor assembly, which instantly disintegrated.

There was a small puff of smoke and the Blackhawk spun toward the ground.

Chapter 2

It was Sunday morning, October 3. Globe, Arizona, native and West Point graduate Lieutenant Larry Perino allowed himself to sleep in until 8:00 A.M. This was unusual for the popular Ranger B company platoon leader who didn't think this day would be any different from any other since he got to Mogadishu last August. In fact, the men of the 3rd Ranger Battalion named each day in this forsaken part of Africa "groundhog day" from the Bill Murray movie where each day was exactly the same as the day before.

Things were about to change.

If anything could make a day in Mogadishu special, Sunday came as close as any for the men of Task Force Ranger. This Sunday they would be served a big dinner. Afterward, the Rangers would play volleyball games, which frequently were quite competitive. Other Rangers spent time writing letters home. Still others worked to stay in top physical condition running laps around the airfield in the desert heat. Every Ranger thought about the day they could leave this forbidding place and return home to Fort Benning, Georgia.

At 1:00 P.M. word spread there might be a mission.

The Company officers were called to the Joint Operations Command Center (JOC) for a briefing. Here some men were already watching live television pictures taken from a supersecret Navy P-3 Orion spy plane flying high over Mogadishu. They watched as a Somali informant parked his car next to a building on a busy street in the "Black Sea" area and then according to the prearranged signal, lifted his hood and walked around the car twice. This signal informed Task Force Ranger leaders, including their tough, cigar-chewing commander, Major General Bill Garrison, who had come to Somalia disguised as a lieutenant colonel, that top Aidid lieutenants and possibly Aidid himself were present.

The operation was set into gear when the "runner" standing at the JOC door was dispatched to the hangar where the rest of the men were waiting for orders to proceed with mission preparation.

Immediately, the men began wrapping their level-three Kevlar bulletproof vests over their desert battle dress utility (BDU) uniforms. These vests were strong enough to stop an AK-47 round, but no one would say they were made for comfort in Mogadishu's blazing desert heat. The men helped themselves to hand grenades, automatic weapons rounds, and then checked their weapons. The entire combat battle load weighed about forty pounds—which actually felt fairly light to this select group of soldiers who regularly trained with heavier loads.

Lieutenant Perino and his company commander from Statham, Georgia, Captain Mike Steele, a deadly serious former offensive lineman for the national champion Georgia Bulldog football team, began briefing the men on the mission. Perino began the mission introduction to his platoon with a map in front of him. "It looks like we have good intell on this target. We have at least two 'tier-one personalities' here. It's going to be a hot party." Then, pointing to his men, Perino warned them, "Any time we go into this area, it's Indian country and we're going to get into a gunfight." He couldn't have been more right.

"Tier-one personalities" were people in Aidid's organization who were considered the most important. In fact, the men of Task Force Ranger had even identified a "top ten hit-list" from this tier-one group. Anyone captured on that list would make any afternoon's work pretty worthwhile.

The operation plan was to have four blocking positions or "chalks" surrounding the target building. These positions would be set up and manned by Rangers. Every light infantryman going into these positions would fast-rope in from one of four Blackhawk helicopters. These helicopters would immediately follow the helicopters carrying the supersecret Delta Force from Fort Bragg, North Carolina, as they landed near—and on—the target building.

Fast-roping out of helicopters was something the men trained for and knew how to do well. The rope they used was a woven nylon rope about 3-1/2 inches in diameter. Every man wore special gloves. It took two seconds going down about forty feet.

The Rangers holding the four blocking positions were to stop anyone coming into or leaving the area while Delta Force cleared the target building and took prisoners. This building-clearing operation by Special Forces soldiers was well rehearsed, quick, efficient, and violent. Taking the building would be quick. The Task Force, with its prisoners in tow, would be out of the area so fast that the rest of Aidid's militia wouldn't know what happened.

Perino's platoon was assigned to enter the area riding in Michael Durant's Super 64 Blackhawk helicopter and hold Chalk Position One at the southeast corner of the target building. The plan was for two Ranger platoons, each divided in half, to create these four blocking chalk positions on each corner of the building. Each squad would consist of seven or eight men, and be led by either an NCO or one of the mission's two platoon leaders, Perino or Lieutenant Tom DiTomasso.

Perino had fifteen men with him in the back of his Super 64 aircraft waiting for the code words that would launch the fleet. Captain Steele, the Bravo company commander, was sitting next to him as was usually the case when the fleet had a mission.

"Radio check, over," one of the four radios crackled for the captain's radioman to hear. "Any questions?" Captain Steele asked Lieutenant Perino. There were none and the men waited until the "Irene" code word was given which would launch the fleet.

Brief, but surprisingly intense boredom was what the men experienced those few minutes in the heat as they sat in the back of their crowded helicopters anticipating combat. That full load of combat gear in their laps didn't help matters much as they waited for their pilot's announcement that the fleet launch word had been given. Sixteen helicopters waited and few men talked. All thought about their jobs and what they might expect in the coming hour.

Finally, pilot Michael Durant's announcement came over the aircraft intercom to the men packed in the back of the Super 64 Blackhawk nicknamed "Viper." Although not eloquent, Durant's message was always delivered the same way. In a softly sung crescendo, the pilot simply reported over the aircraft's intercom, "Fuckin' Irene." These were the words everyone was waiting for. They were on their way.

Lieutenant Perino and Captain Steele smiled slightly at each other and, repeating their own ritual as they had done on their prior six air missions, they gave each other an up and down clenched fist "good luck" high five. Other men tensed their faces and began chanting softly, "Irene. Irene."

The sound of the helicopter fleet was deafening as the powerful helicopters launched from the Mogadishu airport. Another recon aircraft started giving the fleet's lead aircraft piloted by CW5 Randy Jones directions to the target area.

"Give 'em six minutes," Durant said over the intercom to his two crew chiefs, Sergeants Bill Cleveland and Tommie Fields who wore helmet radio gear and monitored all communications. Hearing this, both "Viper" Super 64 chiefs who were tied in at the aircraft's open side doors quickly put up six fingers to signal the Rangers watching them from the back.

The soldiers now began a last check on their gloves and helmets. Finally, Durant reported he had received the "Lucy" code word which ordered the attack to commence. Both crew chiefs raised their thumbs and mouthed "Lucy" to the Rangers and the men knew this would be no dry run.

The adrenaline rushed and the quiet excitement became more intense as the men prepared for battle. "When we got the one-minute warning, we had our game faces on," remembers Larry Perino. "I was facing the tail of the aircraft looking back and there was dust everywhere as we began hovering." The Delta assault force was being inserted by the first team of helicopters who were just ahead of the Ranger blocking force crammed in the four Blackhawks of team two. The Blackhawks waited about a hundred feet up until the dust cleared enough to go lower and release the Rangers to set up the blocking positions.

The architecture of the shacks below them was pretty flimsy. Perino watched as two roofs blew away from the houses around the target building. It looked like a tornado had hit with parts of houses and trash everywhere. It also seemed to the young lieutenant that this part of the operation was lasting longer than it should have.

Finally, Durant's Super 64 Blackhawk came down to thirty feet. The signal to drop the ropes was given. "I could see one of our ropes get caught on some tension wires," remembers Perino. "Fortunately, we pulled forward a little and they released."

Perino looked at his friend Captain Steele and said, "See you man. See you when we get back." He adjusted his radio headset one more time and out the door he dropped.

The rest of the men followed quickly on the ropes to the ground. The three other Blackhawks inserted their Rangers into the assigned "Chalk" holding positions at the three other corners of the building. The Rangers could hear explosions from the center of the target building where Delta Force was already blowing doors open with "flash bang" grenades and taking prisoners.

"Black Six, this is Chalk Four over." The call from the blocking position northwest of the target building was directed to Captain Steele, the Ranger blocking position leader. "Black Six, this is Chalk Four over," the call was repeated, this time betraying some urgency.

Lieutenant Perino was placing his men in their positions and he could see Captain Steele wasn't getting these radio transmissions. "This is Chalk One, go ahead," he replied and then yelled, to his captain. "Sir, you're being called by Chalk Four."

The Rangers of Chalk Four had been inserted at the target building's northwest position. Because of the dust from the helicopters inserting the assault force directly in front of them, this Ranger platoon led by NCO Sergeant Eversman was dropped from a higher altitude about a block away from where they wanted to be. These soldiers couldn't even see the "ground" when they hit the ropes. One of the Chalk Four Rangers, Sergeant Blackburn fell from his rope in the confusion, hit his head, and began to have a seizure.

"We have a casualty," yelled Sergeant Eversman to Lieutenant Perino in the radio. "He's critical. We're treating him, but we need to get him out of here, now."

By now, Captain Steele, whose radio was later discovered to have a bullet in it, was at Lieutenant Perino's side to hear his radio and find out what was going wrong. "Roger. Treat him and get him under cover." There was nothing more Captain Steele could do right now. He knew it wouldn't be long and the Task Force Ranger operation would be completed and they could get out of here. Only then could real medical care be given to the critically injured Ranger.

"We were at our battle positions," remembers Perino. "No one was getting in or out of the target building. Periodically, we saw Special Forces guys cross a window or race up a stairs. Occasionally, dust would billow from a room when a grenade exploded."

The Delta Force soldiers doing their work in the target building were part of an elite, specially trained group. These men knew very well how to take a building and they did it with deadly efficiency. These men, who the army doesn't even admit exist, wore different vests than the Rangers. Theirs were ominous-looking black vests in contrast to the desert colors of the Rangers. The Delta Special Forces helmets were different too, looking more like hockey helmets than combat helmets. Perino knew that anyone dumb enough to resist the black-clad soldiers in the building right now was making a very unhealthy decision.

Outside the building, the enemy fire began immediately but was initially fairly light. However, with each minute it was getting more and more intense. Strangely, the Rangers watched the streets begin to fill with unarmed civilians, mostly women and children, who started walking toward the action.

Perino couldn't be sure where most of the Somali fire was coming from. He was getting pretty uncomfortable watching the women and children walking around.

"Hey, there's a guy with a machine gun right behind that lady!" one of the Rangers yelled, pointing to a small group of people walking toward the blocking position.

"Shoot them, damn it!" ordered Perino. Sergeant Elliott smacked Private First Class Heard on the head and the private let both of the Somalis have it with his M-60 machine gun. "They are gone, sir," reported Heard as Perino turned his head away.

Little could they know then, but death on this day was just beginning. Cliff Wolcott and Donovan Briley were living their final minute.

Chapter 3

Everyone saw Cliff Wolcott's Super 61 Blackhawk go down.

Michael Goffena, a thirtyish, softspoken veteran pilot, who had recently become engaged, was flying the Super 62 Blackhawk. He was Cliff Wolcott's wingman. Both helicopters were 180 degrees apart from each other in a "low cap" altitude of only two hundred feet. The pilots were flying a counterclockwise orbit over the target building and had just finished inserting their assault troops.

No one said it, but every pilot knew it. With all the rocket-propelled grenade fire in the air, it was just a matter of time before helicopters were going to start getting hit.

Earlier that afternoon, Wolcott, the MH-60 Blackhawk assault aircraft leader, had come out of the Tactical Operations Command headquarters at the airport to brief the other Blackhawk helicopter pilots on the mission. So far each Task Force Ranger's mission to capture Aidid or his lieutenants had its own unique characteristics, but this one seemed to have better intelligence.

In fact, the Task Force Ranger commanders believed this mission had more chance for success than any prior one the Task Force had conducted in Mogadishu.

"This is the target building and we'll come in from the north," Wolcott said pointing to the map as he looked up at Goffena. "The gunships are going to make a pass and put in suppressive fire, if needed, before our assault landing will take place."

Wolcott knew what he was talking about because there were few better at their jobs than he. And the other pilots knew it.

He was born in Germany to an army family. Popular in his Richburg, New York, high school, as well as being a power forward on the school's basketball team, Cliff had always been a competitor. He was also deeply patriotic.

When Wolcott graduated from high school in 1975, it was only natural for him to join the army. He went to flight school at Fort Rucker, Alabama, and in 1984, joined the ranks of the best military helicopter pilots in the world. He was accepted into the 160th Special Aviation Regiment.

During his nearly ten years in the regiment, Wolcott distinguished himself. He received numerous awards including a Silver Star for a classified mission during the Gulf War. He also received a Soldier's Medal for saving the life of a co-pilot during a training crash.

The assault team helicopters Wolcott was leading that Sunday in Mogadishu consisted of powerful Blackhawk helicopters. There were eight of them in the sixteen aircraft Task Force Ranger fleet. These helicopters would carry the bulk of the Special Forces troops into the target area.

Blackhawks are ten-ton Sikorsky helicopters with twin 800-horsepower engines. They can easily carry eighteen soldiers fully equipped while speeding toward their targets at over two hundred miles per hour.

Wolcott's pilots had been practicing their insertion techniques at Fort Bragg, North Carolina, for several months before arriving in Somalia on August 26. They had, by now, learned instinctively what they called their "template" or mission choreography. Each helicopter pilot knew exactly where he should go and where he should be at all times during the Special Forces troop insertion, the ground action, and the troop "exfill," or exit and recovery after the mission was completed.

These men were the best the U.S. military had to offer and they were ready for their mission that day. But they could never be ready to have their leader and friend shot out of the air.

Wolcott had just roped his troops into the objective. It took about forty-five seconds for everyone to leave the aircraft. Two Special Forces snipers and Wolcott's two crew chiefs stayed on board.

"There was so much noise and activity that day," remembers wingman Goffena in the Super 62 Blackhawk. "Imagine the shake of sixteen combat aircraft on top of you. And then, all of a sudden, the visibility goes to zero from kicked-up dust as the helicopters started coming down."

The roads around the target were just dirt, and with the incredible rotor wash from the aircraft, a giant dust cloud began rising up and obscuring anything in its path. Some of the buildings began to collapse from the backwash as assault helicopters lifted off after inserting the Delta Force. Goffena and Wolcott's aircraft stayed close to the ground, initiating a counterclockwise overwatch pattern looking for targets which might hinder the troops now on the ground.

The ground fire increased almost immediately. The pilots knew that things were going to get more entertaining fairly soon.

Somalis began shooting their AK-47 rifles while a few others began engaging with 30-caliber machine guns. The 7.62 miniguns in the doors of the Blackhawks began to heat up as the exchange started to even.

"The Somalis were a curious bunch," remembers Goffena. "For every armed person, there were fifty unarmed just standing around, often right next to the guy firing at us."

The helicopter gunners soon discovered that by laying a short burst of fire at the feet of these crowds, the unarmed people would drop first with just an instant of delay before the armed person dropped to the ground.

This was the advantage the helicopter gunners needed. They began to repeatedly take advantage of the short moment when the only person standing was the armed person. Somali ground gunners started getting "stitched up" with this technique.

It wasn't long before rocket-propelled grenade fire began to increase. When the words, "Blackhawk going down," came over the radio, Michael Goffena knew it had to be his friend and wingman, Cliff Wolcott.

Dan Jollota flying high overhead in the Combat Search and Rescue Blackhawk (CSAR) heard the transmission and looked down to see Wolcott's aircraft spinning with parts flying in every direction. Then, he saw the aircraft go into the ground, hard.

Jollota figured things didn't look too good for the crew of Wolcott's helicopter, but he knew he was going down to help. He quickly radioed to the back of his helicopter, "An aircraft is down. Prepare for insertion." The men in his Search and Rescue helicopter had trained extensively for this situation and they knew exactly what to do in a crash situation.

Sergeant First Class Al Lamb, the CSAR insertion team leader in the back of Jollota's aircraft reported to the men, "We have a bird down. We don't know which one yet or how many casualties."

Instantly, the eleven crash site security specialists and four trauma medics began preparation for insertion. The troops checked their gloves and then pulled back their weapon handles to make sure they were locked and loaded with magazines in the chamber.

Sergeant Mark Belda, one of the weapons team members sitting on the left side of the CSAR aircraft could occasionally catch a glimpse of the battle. He remembers, "We kept flying in circles and just waiting for the orders to go do it."

Then, SFC Lamb was on the aircraft intercom again, saying, "I don't know exactly where the crash is. We're going to follow another bird in. We're on our way in."

Immediately after the crash occurred, Wolcott's wingman Michael Goffena in the Super 62 Blackhawk helicopter, was over the crash site. He began laying suppressive fire to keep armed Somalis and the legions of unarmed curious, but dangerous, civilians away. This was rapidly becoming an unsuccessful and impossible task.

Almost immediately after the crash, Chief Warrant Officers Karl Maier and Keith Jones in the STAR 41 little bird MH-6 gunship were landing their helicopter just behind Wolcott's crashed helicopter in a narrow alley facing west. This alley was so narrow there were no more than two feet separating each rotor blade from the alleyway walls as the helicopter came down.

After landing, Jones could see that there were people still alive from the crashed aircraft who were not going to make it on their own to the safety of his little bird helicopter. Instinctively, in one of the most daring actions of the day, Jones left the protection of his helicopter while under fire and started toward the crashed helicopter.

Immediately, he saw two badly injured crewmen who were trying to crawl toward him. He grabbed the most seriously injured soldier who was already being dragged toward the helicopter gunship by another injured crew member. Quickly Jones helped both men back toward the intersection which was becoming the focus of the Somali attack.

By now, the other pilot, Karl Maier, was firing his hand weapon out the door of the waiting aircraft and a dead Somali was already lying next to him. It was clear the Somali militia were concentrating their fire on this rescue as the injured men were quickly placed in the back of the STAR aircraft. The little bird took off just as Jollota's rescue aircraft came dropping toward the crash site.

Everyone always hoped that Dan Jollota's Search and Rescue helicopter would never have to be used, but when it was needed, it sure was nice to have. Jollota, married with an eighteen-month-old son, had already been in the army for eighteen years. His men were experts at crash site security and medical rescue. The rescue team prepared to fast-rope into the crash site because there wasn't anywhere to land such a large helicopter.

As he got closer, Jollota saw some movement in the back of Wolcott's aircraft, which was laying on its side in an alley. The rotors were separated from the rest of the wreckage and the cockpit was jammed into a wall. There was no movement from the badly twisted helicopter, which had surprisingly not burst into flames on impact.

Jollota could see that Cliff Wolcott's thirty-three-year-old co-pilot, Donovan Briley from North Little Rock, Arkansas, was dead. He wasn't sure about Wolcott yet.

Sergeant Mark Belda remembers, "We started into the battle zone and went into a hover. When the aircraft flared, we instantly had two ropes out of the helicopter and we started down."

Maier and Jones's STAR 41 little bird was taking off just as Jollota's Combat Search and Rescue helicopter arrived. The CSAR team immediately began fast-roping in from thirty-one feet in the air.

As this was happening, Jollota's crew watched what turned out to be a badly injured Special Forces soldier from the crashed helicopter defending the intersection directly behind the downed helicopter. This soldier was alone and had earlier refused his own personal rescue from the STAR little bird helicopter. In fact, he continued to refuse help and remained on post at the intersection until well after the other rescue troops had arrived.

As the Search and Rescue helicopter was completing the rescue team insertion, the aircraft door gunners became extremely active providing cover fire.

Then Jollota heard a loud crash and explosion from the left side of his aircraft. Immediately he knew his Blackhawk was hit and reflexively started to pull in power to lift out.

One of the crew chiefs from the back yelled, "We still have people on the ropes." In fact, the last four Special Forces soldiers were still roping down.

Jollota checked the controllability of the aircraft, and continued to hover until his ropes were clear. The Super 68 Blackhawk started struggling out of the area.

Goffena, flying next to Jollota's rescue aircraft, saw the RPG hit. He remembers, "I couldn't believe the discipline Jollota showed as he continued to hover with people on his ropes despite the fact he had just been blasted. Every pilot's training and reflexes are to start moving after being hit."

Super 68's blades started whistling from holes and dents made from shattered metal. Jollota knew his aircraft had taken an RPG hit somewhere.

"The aircraft started to slosh," Jollota remembers. "I scanned the instruments and knew we were severely damaged. I didn't know how badly we were hit, but I figured it was pretty bad."

Hal Ward in the lead little bird gun ship also saw the Search and Rescue aircraft blasted and remembers, "It didn't look good. I'll tell you, we thought he was going in."

The grenade blast had blown into the aircraft's main rotor system and the cooler system had been destroyed. Light puffs of smoke started coming from the aircraft and Ward quickly reported this to Jollota who now had his hands full.

An aircraft above saw how badly damaged the Search and Rescue craft was and radioed, "Super Six Eight, you have severe damage. Land immediately."

This was followed almost immediately by the Air Mission Commander Lieutenant Colonel Tom Matthews in the high overhead Command and Control aircraft telling Jollota to make his own decision about whether he could make it back to a safe area or not.

Jollota began having quite a bit of difficulty controlling his aircraft. It felt like driving a car on a frozen lake. He decided to attempt a landing at a small field he had seen earlier in the afternoon. It was just a kilometer away, but he wasn't sure his aircraft would hold up to let him make it there. Blackhawk helicopters were designed to run for a few minutes without any lubrication, but the lack of a cooling system was another matter.

Jollota's co-pilot reported that the engine was holding up and the amazing aircraft kept flying.

After what seemed like an eternity, they made it to the open field. Now, Jollota decided that, since they were still flying, they might have a better chance if they just kept going and tried to make it all the way back to the airfield.

The decision was made and they were going to try.

Jollota radioed into the Mogadishu tower, "Mog tower, this is Super Six Eight. Alert crash rescue to meet us. We're coming in hard."

The pilot started discussing emergency landing procedures with his crew. They knew they wouldn't last much longer in the air. When the airfield came into sight, everyone took a deep breath and held it. Jollota knew his helicopter would never survive a hover landing so he shot in with a 60-knot straight-in roll right on the landing skids.

They made it.

On the ground, Jollota and his crew wanted to immediately get back into the action. They found the company's maintenance test pilot and discussed how they could get the only spare Blackhawk into some kind of flying condition.

The mechanics got to work preparing the spare helicopter, which had just received a new engine. Jollota and his crew started transferring their crashed aircraft's Personnel Locator System (PLS) to the spare Blackhawk. The PLS was a special receiver used to locate a downed pilot's location from signals given from small transmitters located in pilot flight suits.

Jollota had a feeling that the PLS was going to be an important piece of equipment to have. Within an hour he and his crew were in the air in the backup helicopter.

Unfortunately, Jollota's feeling was right. They spent the next eighteen hours looking for crewmen of still another aircraft which had just been shot down and was about to be overrun by Somali gunmen.

Chapter 4

The Delta assault force had taken its building and held prisoners. The Rangers were holding the blocking positions around the building. The helicopters were still overhead providing support fire. Wolcott's helicopter hadn't been hit yet and, except for a Ranger fast-rope injury, the action was going pretty much according to the Task Force's plan.

Lieutenant Colonel Tom Matthews in the Command and Control helicopter knew that with all the RPG fire in the air, the helicopters were at an ever increasing risk the longer the operation lasted. Everyone was waiting for the code word, "Laurie" to be passed over the radio net so they could get out.

When it finally came, everyone knew the target building had been secured and the prisoners were ready to be loaded onto trucks. The trip back to the Task Force Ranger base at the Mogadishu airport would begin soon. Maybe, just in time.

Lieutenant Perino felt some relief when he heard the "Laurie" code word, but he knew there was still some more time needed before they could move out. The mission hadn't felt right to him from the beginning. He was anxious to get out of there.

He wondered how much longer it would be.

Five minutes went by and he could see the Delta Force soldiers still getting their "flex tied" prisoners out of the building and loaded into the five-ton trucks. These trucks, driven by Rangers, had moved surreptitiously into the "Black Sea" area after the Task Force landed. The drivers had been nervously waiting themselves—about two hundred meters to the south—for the signal to come in to load up the prisoners and Task Force soldiers, and then get out as quickly as they could.

Precious minutes were passing.

Then the entire mission changed. The terrible words filled everyone's radios, "Aircraft hit. Aircraft hit."

Perino muttered to himself, "Oh shit." He touched Captain Steele on the shoulder and said, "An aircraft just got shot down." To the northeast they both watched Cliff Wolcott's aircraft spin into the ground.

Perino began passing word to all other blocking positions that an aircraft was down. His conscientiousness was probably unnecessary because most of the Americans saw the same bone-chilling sight.

Lieutenant Tom DiTomasso, a handsome young lieutenant from Rhode Island, was the platoon leader of blocking position Number Two at the northeast corner of the assault building. His position was the closest to where Wolcott went down.

DiTomasso's fifteen Rangers had been engaging a large crowd of armed Somalis north of their position. Additionally, the Ranger had just found four Mercedes Benz automobiles hidden in an alley. These vehicles belonged to Aidid's lieutenants—the targets of the mission. They were being guarded by four drivers who happened to be throwing hand grenades at the Ranger position. Three of these men were quickly captured. The fourth was killed as he resisted.

When DiTomasso saw Wolcott's crash, he realized that he needed to act quickly if any survivors of the crash were to make it through alive. He knew the crash site would soon be overtaken by the same armed Somalian mob the Rangers had been engaging to the north.

He ordered three of his fifteen men to hold the prisoners and the blocking position with machine guns. Without hesitation he began running with his Ranger platoon in the direction of the downed aircraft.

The young Lieutenant could see a crowd of armed Somalis a block away leave their positions also. He knew the Somalis were also headed to the crash site. It would be a race to see who could get there first.

DiTomasso's twelve Rangers ran down unsecured and unfamiliar streets, firing their weapons to open a path. They ran down narrow alleys deeper and deeper into "bandit territory" toward a destination that seemed like miles away, even though it was actually only six hundred yards away. The Rangers could hear—and sometimes see—helicopter gunships directly over them trying to help.

Karl Maier and Keith Jones had landed their little bird gun ship at the crash site. Jones was already outside the aircraft completely exposed looking for survivors.

Rounding a corner DiTomasso found himself looking directly at the nose of Maier's STAR 41 gunship. Karl Maier was ready to shoot him. Maier had his right foot outside the aircraft and he was aiming his automatic weapon. A dead Somali was already laying near his aircraft. A steady stream of fire was continuing to spray the area.

"He pointed his weapon at me and, at the last second, realized we were Rangers," remembers Lieutenant DiTomasso. "When he put his weapon down, I signaled to him by tapping my helmet. I wanted a head count on how many men were injured."

Maier did not know for sure how many were still alive, but he pointed to the rear to let DiTomasso know there were still people in Wolcott's crashed aircraft at the intersection just behind him. DiTomasso could see co-pilot Keith Jones and another wounded soldier dragging an unconscious crew member from the crashed helicopter toward his little bird aircraft.

DiTomasso began directing his men into security positions around the crash site. He sent his medic straight into the crashed helicopter as Maier's little bird took off with the only two injured men they could extract from the crash. Almost immediately, Dan Jollota's Search and Rescue helicopter came overhead and began roping their fifteen-man crash security team in.

Reporting back to Captain Steele, Lieutenant DiTomasso said, "Chalk Four at crash site. Hard hit. Six hurt." Six Rangers were shot already and DiTomasso knew he was in the fight of his life.

Sergeant John Belman, one of the Combat Search and Rescue (CSAR) soldiers in Jollota's Super 68 Blackhawk remembers, "We roped in from about forty-five feet. We've done it a thousand times in training and it takes about three seconds to get down from that height. We could see the other Ranger element arriving and the little bird taking off just as we got there."

On the ground, Belman's pre-arranged responsibility was the six o'clock position near the crashed aircraft; the nose was twelve o'clock. The Rangers could see that there were two crewmen from the crash still alive on the ground. One was a Special Forces sniper and the other one of the crew chiefs.

The Special Forces sniper had been shot in the face but had struggled out of his crashed aircraft. He had helped an injured crewman to Maier and Jones's aircraft; he was still trying to fight. He was obviously hurt pretty badly. His face was bloody and he could barely walk because of compression fractures in his back.

Belman ran over to him and started dragging him out of the open to shield him from the enemy fire. He helped the wounded Special Forces soldier to a safer position at the rear of the crashed aircraft. After firing his rifle, Belman turned around to see how the injured man was doing. The sniper was gone.

Belman looked out to see him crawling through the enemy fire to the intersection where he began firing his weapon again.

Another soldier, Specialist Stebbins, was defending the intersection—now the main Somali attack point. It would be through this intersection that the trapped Rangers would be overrun if they couldn't hold the Somalis off. Everyone could see Stebbins had become a target. He continued to fire his weapon. But the enemy soldiers were firing back and they were gathering strength.

Belman watched as Stebbins got hit in the chest and went down. "I thought he was dead," remembers Belman. "Then, I watched him get up and start shooting again. Then incredibly, he was hit again and down he went, only to stand up a second time and begin shooting his weapon as if nothing had happened." Stebbins was being hit in his chest protective vest, but he wouldn't move from his position. And he wouldn't stop fighting.

By now, several medics were working inside the aircraft where they could see that both pilots, Cliff Wolcott and Donovan Briley, were dead. Briley had received three bullet wounds in his back and another wound to his neck. The head pilot, Cliff Wolcott, was crushed on impact and was now tightly pinned in the cockpit.

"Let's pull out these mats from the floor," said one of the medics to Belman. Immediately the Kevlar floorboards of the crashed aircraft were pulled out and set up to provide some protection for the people trying to get the dead pilots out. The fire from the Somalis around the area was getting more and more intense as the gunmen realized the main group of Americans were now grouping near the aircraft.

Sergeant Belman realized he had to get the wounded under more cover or all of them would eventually be picked off. He saw a hole in the wall that the helicopter made when it crashed. "Let's try to get some of the wounded in there," Belman said to one of the CSAR radiomen.

They were able to get two wounded into the hole before the radioman was shot in the back. Belman moved his hand grenades out of his pocket. He didn't want to take a hit and have them explode. He continued moving wounded into the hole until the fire became so intense everyone had to stop moving until the protection of darkness came.

The little bird gunships kept up a steady stream of fire, trying to keep the Somalis from overrunning the Americans whose position was quite unstable. The rest of the Task Force Ranger soldiers were now fighting their way toward the crash site. Fewer and fewer were fighting as the casualties increased.

The Somali fire was so intense that the wounded could not be moved. Everyone just lay where they fell. All they could do now was wait. The Rangers hoped a rescue operation would arrive soon or darkness would come in time to give enough concealment to regroup. Attempting to reorganize the team now was foolish.

Back at the target building, the prisoners had been loaded into the trucks. This truck convoy, led by Lieutenant Colonel Danny McKnight, would take a northern route along major roads toward the crash site. The rest of the blocking Rangers—and most of the assault Delta Force—were fighting on foot directly toward the crash site. They knew they would be desperately needed there.

Unfortunately, the convoy would soon encounter disaster. The trucks would be forced to turn back.

Chapter 5

Sergeant Bill Powell from Galesburg, Illinois, had been in the army for sixteen years and a Ranger for seven. He was in charge of the convoy's fire support team.

He was in the third vehicle of the convoy ground force led by Lieutenant Colonel Dan McKnight. Their mission was to follow the air assault forces and be ready to extract them and their prisoners for a quick dash back to base after the mission was completed.

When the Task Force Ranger helicopter fleet left the airfield on the mission, so did the ground contingent which consisted of ten vehicles. The Command and Control airship was able to follow the convoy by tracking the large fluorescent orange "VS-17" panels placed on the trucks' roofs.

It took the ground forces thirteen minutes to get to a position just two hundred meters from the target house. Here, they waited until the "Laurie" code word was given. "Laurie" was the signal to come in and load up prisoners. When "Laurie" was given, the ground convoy started forward. The Rangers got out of their vehicles and walked along the side of the road to the target house.

Private First Class Tory Carlson from Scottsdale, Arizona, turned a corner just in time to see Corporal James Cavaco from Forestdale, Massachusetts, get hit in the head. Cavaco was a Mark-19 gunner manning an automatic weapon mounted on one of the vehicles. He was shot and he fell over his turret. One of the Special Forces soldiers saw it too and shouted, "He's dead. He's fuckin' dead. Just put him in the vehicle. Let's go."

Loading the prisoners took almost thirty minutes. During that time the convoy was taking fire from the alleys and windows.

While the prisoners were loaded, Sergeant Powell had moved into an alleyway with two Special Forces soldiers to suppress some Somali sniper fire. The soldiers were pinned down by Somali gunmen from both sides of a street. Just as the soldiers turned to make a break toward their truck, an RPG struck the ground behind them. Powell was hit in both legs. One of the Special Forces soldiers was knocked to the ground. All three crawled into some nearby bushes. They began to return fire down an alley.

Lieutenant Colonel McKnight yelled, "Sergeant Powell. Sergeant Powell. Get back here if you can." The men made another dash and Powell was wounded in the leg yet again. But this time the men reached the vehicle.

"Let it go, let's get out of here," shouted Powell to McKnight. As the troops fired through the Humvee windows, the vehicles raced out of the area with their prisoners.

Powell bled as he fired his rifle. Several dead soldiers lay in the trucks ahead and many more wounded were piled up alongside with the "hog-tied" prisoners.

The convoy proceeded up a block from the target house and made a right-hand turn. They were trying to find their way to Wolcott's crash site. Everyone had orders to meet at the crash if they could get there.

After a few more turns, the convoy found themselves in a dusty alley leading nowhere. A large dirt mound stood before the convoy. Somali weapons fire increased. Lieutenant Colonel McKnight took shrapnel in the neck. Wounded, he ordered the convoy to back out of there—and quick.

Trying a different approach, McKnight saw the paved Armed Forces Road and the convoy made a dash there. Sergeant Pringle was manning a 50-caliber machine gun when he saw four men running away with an RPG launcher. By now, everyone was getting a little tired of RPGs and Pringle ripped into them with an effective vengeance.

The convoy passed another building from which people were firing. Sergeant Pringle returned the fire and blanketed the building with shots from his automatic weapon. Still, the convoy couldn't find the crash site. And in the confusion the helicopter gunships lost the convoy. A helicopter gunship requested the convoy to shoot up a flare. Immediately, a violet smoke canister flared upward from one of the trucks.

The helicopter instructed the convoy to go two blocks south and then turn left.

Quickly complying, the convoy made a U-turn. It drove right into a Somali ambush. There were sixty-five Task Force soldiers and twenty prisoners in the seven vehicles left. There were at least twenty wounded Americans with three dead and Sergeant Lorenzo Ruiz from El Paso, Texas, was near death.

A fierce firefight followed with intense weapons fire from both sides. The third vehicle in the convoy was destroyed by a direct RPG hit.

The two vehicles at the front of the convoy sped up, trying to escape the kill zone. They thought the trucks behind were trying to do the same. But the rest of the convoy was stopped. They were trapped behind the third vehicle, which was in flames. And they were taking a beating.

When the two lead vehicles realized the convoy had been stopped, Sergeant Bob Galleher—in the second vehicle—pulled up beside Powell, who was now in the first vehicle, and together, they made the decision to go back.

They returned to the ambush site where an intense battle was raging. Powell remembers, "By the time we returned, casualties littered the street. I heard a loud boom and looked back. Rodriguez and the three soldiers sitting next to him were blown from our vehicle. Everyone in our Humvee was injured now except for our driver."

At this point, over forty of the sixty-five men in the convoy were wounded. Lieutenant Colonel McKnight, who had the responsibility for the prisoners, knew they were the primary objective of the mission. A decision had to be made.

McKnight remembers, "I had lost three vehicles, including two five-ton trucks. We had very little ammunition left and I was cramming people into the few vehicles I had left. In addition, I had numerous casualties including the three men—bodies of Cavaco, Kowaleski, and Joyce—were dead. I didn't want any more."

McKnight knew that even if he got to the crash site, with so many injured, his convoy would become a liability rather than an asset. "By now, I had more casualties than they had."

McKnight knew what he had to do.

"Atom Six Four, this is Uniform Six Four," McKnight called on his radio to Major General William Garrison back at the Mogadishu Airport TOC head-quarters. "We have lost another five ton and we have numerous casualties. I need to return with the casualties and the detainees in the vehicles I have left."

"Roger, Uniform Six Four," was the immediate reply. It was impossible for the convoy to reach and remove the Rangers who were now arriving at Wolcott's Crash Site One.

Quickly, McKnight ordered one of his sergeants who was still functioning, Aaron Weaver, to take the lead vehicle and move out. "Head down Armed Forces Road to Via Linen and then back to the K-4 circle and back to the compound from there. I'll take the rear vehicle. Let's get out of here."

Time was warp speed for the men as the convoy raced out of hell. Many vehicles had their tires shot out. The journey was like running a gauntlet. "We shot our way the entire way home," remembers Sergeant Powell.

The convoy arrived at the K-4 circle a little after 6 P.M. At the K-4 circle, they rendezvoused with Sergeant Mark Warner and a composite band of Rangers who had spent the past two hours trying to fight their way in to help. Lieutenant Colonel McKnight ordered them to turn around. Further action was pointless. They would just be killed if they went any farther in their open vehicles.

They arrived back at the airfield at 6:18 P.M. At that moment, the Rangers at Crash Site One were hunkering down for the night. Michael Durant's Crash Site Two had already been overrun.

Chapter 6

Lieutenant Larry Perino and his Rangers were holding blocking position Number One on the southeast side of the assault house. They waited until the prisoners had been taken from the house by the Delta assault force and loaded into Lieutenant Colonel McKnight's trucks. By now, everyone knew that a helicopter had been shot down. Mission orders had been changed because of the crash.

The new orders were to proceed to Crash Site One and secure the site. Perino didn't know it yet, but a major battle was going on at Crash Site One between a crowd of Somalis and Lieutenant Tom DiTomasso's newly arrived Rangers. Fifteen members of the Combat Search and Rescue (CSAR) team were preparing to drop in to the site from Dan Jollota's Blackhawk helicopter. No one knew what to expect.

In the CSAR helicopter forty-five feet over Wolcott's crash site, Sergeant John Belman was preparing to conduct the rescue operations he and his men had practiced hundreds of time. A little bird helicopter piloted by Karl Maier and Keith Jones had just taken off with two critically injured crew members from Wolcott's crashed helicopter. Two more were still alive on the ground. One was trapped in the aircraft.

These men wouldn't be alone for long.

One of the soldiers left behind was a Special Forces sniper who had been shot in the face, as well as the back and neck. He refused to leave with the little bird helicopter.

"We started into the battle zone and went into a hover," remembers Sergeant Mark Belda, the fire control team leader in the CSAR aircraft. "When the aircraft flared, we instantly had two ropes down."

The fifteen specially trained rescue and medical troops of Dan Jollota's Search and Rescue helicopter were on the ground in seconds. The last four men were still on ropes—jumping from the big Blackhawk—when an RPG sailed into its rotor. There was a jolt. But Jollota held his helicopter in position until the men were down. The Blackhawk limped away with smoke trailing from its rear.

On the ground, the team found and surrounded the crashed helicopter. The fire-control teams established a security perimeter while the medics started work on the injured. Two medics were quickly inside the crashed helicopter working on the single living crewman still trapped inside.

Lieutenant DiTomasso's men had just arrived. The Americans could see a crowd of Somalis two blocks to the north.

The tail of the aircraft was pointing toward an intersection. It had made a gigantic hole in the wall of one of the buildings with the cockpit as it was spinning to the ground. The aircraft was sitting on its left side. Both pilots were obviously dead. The injured sniper could see that medical attention was being given to the injured crew chief, so he limped toward the intersection to help set up a defensive position for the coming battle.

"We started to receive some pretty good fire," remembers Sergeant Belda. "Two of our medics were shot near the aircraft. In fact, within minutes, five of our fifteen-man team had been shot. We started dragging people through the hole made in the wall by the crashed aircraft."

An RPG hit the top of the building directly over Sergeant Belda. Debris flew on top of him, spraying the street as well. Hand grenades started coming over the six-foot walls that encircled the Americans and their crashed helicopter.

Sergeant Belda watched one Somali grenade fly right into the crashed aircraft. He yelled, "Grenade in the copter!" as he and Sergeant Lamb dived into a doorway. He knew the whole aircraft with fuel cells and ammunition was about to go up. But there was nothing he could do about it. The whole alley was going to be blown. He was sure everyone was going to be killed. He leaned against the wall and tensed for the blast.

"I can't believe that thing didn't explode," Sergeant Lamb whispered to Belda. Lamb's lips were only inches away from Belda's ears as the two crouched men waited for their doom.

Fortunately for the Americans, the Somali weapons and ammunition were very old. At that moment, Lamb and Belda realized the benefits of enemy weapons filled with old gunpowder.

Sergeant Belman crawled through the fire to the helicopter and started pulling up the Kevlar floorboards. These would provide some protection for the people working around the aircraft. Another burst of enemy fire had him dive right on top of the dead co-pilot, Donovan Briley, whose body had been dragged outside to the rear of the helicopter. A soldier directly behind Belman was shot in the leg.

Belman looked ahead. Sergeant Lamb, who had dived for cover with him said, "He's got to be in there," pointing forward to a tree about forty meters away. Belman immediately unloaded a 5.56 magazine from his M-16 into the tree. Lamb started laughing. The tree had become a splintered stalk of wood. Belman remembers, "If I didn't get that sniper, I sure scared the shit out of him."

A short time later, Belman remembers a Somalian who was either incredibly brave or incredibly stupid. He stuck his AK-47 around a wall close to where Belman and Lamb had dived for cover. Belman and Lamb watched. They waited for the head to appear, which it soon did. The man's whole upper torso came into view looking for a target.

"We couldn't believe this guy," remembers Belman. "We hesitated for an instant. Then Lamb and I hosed him. We must have gotten off two hundred rounds."

The trapped soldiers could hear firing in the distance. They knew some-one—other Rangers or perhaps the Quick Reaction Force—were trying desperately to rescue them.

Somali fire was so intense now that the wounded could no longer be moved. About half of the forward troops had either been shot or were pinned down either at the aircraft or in the alleyways around the crash. Everyone just lay where they were and hoped dark would come before they were killed.

Back at the assault building, the rest of the Ranger force followed Lieutenant Perino and his men on their dangerous trek to the crash site.

"We crossed the street from the assault house and began fighting our way house-to-house right into the enemy fire," remembers Lieutenant Perino, the platoon leader of blocking position Number One. "We were meeting heavy resistance and grenades started falling into the streets around us."

Perino's ground force, led by Captain Steele, consisted of about thirty Rangers from two blocking positions and the forty Delta assault soldiers, who had just exited the target building.

By now, Lieutenant Colonel McKnight's trucks were loaded and moving out. The truck convoy picked up the Rangers from blocking position Number Four and started to the crash site by a different route. They eventually got lost and suffering casualties were forced to turn back and fight their way to the airfield instead.

Captain Steele's ground forces had problems too. They were having difficulty finding the crash. The Rangers weren't sure where the crash site was. They had seen Wolcott's aircraft go down, but they didn't know which of the dirty, unmarked streets of the Mogadishu slums would take them there. Helicopters overhead danced around the ground fire as they tried to direct the ground force in the right direction.

After about a half hour Perino knew they were getting pretty close to the crash site. "God damnit, I'm hit," yelled Sergeant Williamson. It was a minor wound and a medic quickly assisted him to cover. The ground force kept inching forward.

Turning a corner, Perino saw a large crowd of Somalis to the north. They commenced firing immediately. "Can you see 'em yet?" Perino asked his sergeant, hoping they were about to link up with his friend and fellow platoon leader, Lieutenant Tom DiTomasso. "Not yet," was the reply from Sergeant Elliott, the force's point man.

Perino looked behind him. He could see that a large number of men were already hit. He turned to tell Corporal James Smith from Long Valley, New Jersey, to start firing his M-203 grenade launcher just as the twenty-one-year-old Ranger yelled, "I'm hit! Damnit. I'm hit!"

"Where?" Perino quickly asked.

"Right in the ass," Smith replied.

Perino could see that Smith had a serious wound. The Ranger couldn't move his leg and he was bleeding profusely. Several Rangers moved up and dragged him behind a foundation for cover. Bullets began snapping. The lead troops watched in horror as Sergeant First Class Earl Fillmore from Blairsville, Pennsylvania, got hit. He went down immediately.

"He took a bullet right in the head," remembers Perino. "He fell like a rag doll. I think he was dead before he hit the ground."

Enemy fire intensified as the troops paused. Elliott and Perino were at the very front. They were the most exposed.

As bullets pinged against the wall they were crouched against, Sergeant Elliott turned to his lieutenant and said, "Sir, I think it would be a good idea for us to go over this wall." Perino looked back at his sergeant and in the same calm voice said, "Yes, I think you're right." Both men made a head long dive over the wall for cover.

An instant later, Perino watched as enemy gunners took aim at Specialist Stebbins. He scrambled for cover. When he was hit, he screamed in pain and went over the wall.

"Sergeant Boorn," Perino yelled pointing at his sergeant. "Hey, they're shooting at you! Get down!" Boorn didn't hear his lieutenant. He was shoved out of the line of fire by Specialist Rodriguez, as both men were hit. Boorn, who had a painful leg wound, started to help Rodriguez, the man who had just saved his life. Troopers from Delta leapt out and pulled both into a nearby building.

Lieutenant Perino was fifty yards in front of the rest of the seventy men in the ground force. He realized they were within a block of the crash site. He also knew that to move any farther would be foolish. "We need to strong point (take over) a building here," Perino called back to Captain Steele. "Right now, we need to secure the outside of a building and then strong point the building for protection."

"Roger. Go ahead and secure the closest building," was Captain Steele's quick reply. Steele knew they were close to the crash site because he could hear the fire fight from the helicopter's defenders. But it was getting dark. He thought it too dangerous to go any closer.

By now the seventy-man force had been divided into four informal sections. Each section took a building and set up its own Casualty Collection Points for the numerous wounded men. Eight of the twelve men with Perino in the lead section had been shot. Many of the thirty-three men with Captain Steele had also been wounded.

Lieutenant Perino knew that Specialist Smith was dying. The young soldier kept losing blood. Nothing the three soldiers did stopped the bleeding. And the medics were running out of IV fluids.

"This really hurts," Smith kept telling his lieutenant. "You're going to be all right. We'll get you out of here," lied Perino.

Perino got on the radio and reported the situation to Captain Steele, "Smith is bleeding real bad. He's critical. We need to evacuate him now."

"Stand by," was the captain's reply to Perino. He got on his own radio network and pleaded for a medevac helicopter. In the Command and Control helicopter high above the action, the commanders knew exactly what was going on with Smith, but they also knew that another helicopter had just been shot down. Right now it was too dangerous to send yet another helicopter into the chaotic struggle below.

"Ground forces are on the way," was the only word given to the captain, who didn't think they would arrive in sufficient strength or quick enough.

Within minutes, Perino was on the radio again to his captain, "We need to get Smith out of here now," he said, more in fear than anger.

Again Captain Steele replied "Stand by," and called the Command and Control aircraft again. "We can't bring another bird in" was the terse reply. "The QRF is on the way."

Perino knew that Smith was going to die. But he called a third time to say, "We have to evacuate him now. Do you realize he's not going to make it unless we evacuate now?"

Steele understood. He replied solemnly, "Roger, I understand."

Within minutes, the trapped Rangers started CPR on their comrade. Perino walked out of the room. A minute later he heard the Special Forces medic say, "Hey sir, don't worry about the medevac. It's too late now."

It was getting dark. Just a block down the street from Lieutenant Perino, Lieutenant DiTomasso and his men started crawling back into the streets to pull wounded soldiers to cover. These soldiers had been trapped for several hours, held down by the never-ending Somali fire.

Sergeant Belman from the Search and Rescue team had been trapped on top of Donovan Briley, the dead co-pilot's body for a long time. When he saw Lieutenant DiTomasso venture into the streets, he started to drag the wounded into the huge hole in the wall next to the crashed helicopter.

Almost immediately, he was shot in the buttocks. Realizing he wasn't seriously injured, he pulled the hand grenades out of his back pocket so they wouldn't be hit and explode. Then he resumed dragging the wounded into the hole and the safety it could provide.

When they got into the hole, they blew another hole through a wall. Then they walked into an adjacent living room where they started to gather the casualties for treatment.

Outside, Specialist Stebbins, who had been shot earlier, continued to fight. Several Rangers watched with amazement. As he fired his 203 automatic weapon, he was hit in the chest. He went down and everyone thought he was dead. Then, they watched him stand up and start firing his weapon again, only to be hit in the chest and go down a second time. Again, he stood up, brushed himself off, and started firing again.

Lieutenant Perino, like the rest of the men, wondered how much longer they would be able to hold out. The lieutenant called on his radio again and again to ask his commander and close friend Captain Steele, "Hey sir, what's the status of that QRF? What the hell is going on?"

Each time Captain Steele, realizing the frustration of his men, would reply facetiously, "It's O.K. They just left. They'll be here in a minute." This reply, repeated over and over, relieved the tension because neither Steele nor Perino no longer believed the reports that the QRF would be there soon. Once during those early evening hours of darkness, Captain Steele called his lieutenant for a status report. Before he could say anything, Perino broke in and said, "No, don't tell me. They'll be here in a minute, right?" Both men laughed.

Throughout the early evening, the little bird helicopters kept up relentless fire on the Somali positions. "Those little birds saved our lives," remembers Steele. "They were firing so close we actually felt their cartridges hit our helmets."

Once, the fire control officer, Sergeant Goodale, was told by one of the little birds, "There are about fifteen people moving toward your position." Then, all of a sudden, helicopters appeared from nowhere and blanketed the area immediately in front of the crashed helicopter with a solid wall of fire. Repeatedly, the helicopters cleared the streets of Somali attackers.

It was indeed fortunate the helicopters were there because the trapped soldiers were not only running out of medical supplies and water, they were also getting low on ammunition. Captain Steele ordered, "Let's save our last IV fluid for the next man that goes into shock."

The men could hear battle sounds in the distance. They knew their Ranger comrades as well as units from the 10th Mountain Quick Reaction Force were trying desperately to get to them. It was probably good that the trapped soldiers couldn't know how long they would take.

Chapter 7

Lieutenant Colonel Tom Matthews, the Air Mission Commander in the Command and Control Blackhawk flying high over the action, watched as Cliff Wolcott's Super 61 helicopter spun to the ground. In the dust and death below, the character of the mission had just changed dramatically.

Matthews immediately ordered Karl Maier and Keith Jones in their STAR 44 little bird to the crash site. He watched them attempt a daring rescue of the injured crewmen from Wolcott's downed aircraft. He saw Dan Jollota's Search and Rescue Blackhawk helicopter discharge troops on ropes to provide crash-site security and medical support. He saw the aircraft take a hit and watched it exude smoke on the way back to the airfield.

No one knew that both pilots in Wolcott's Super 61 were dead. But Rangers fighting their way toward the crash site would not have paused in their efforts in any case. The Ranger Creed, known by every Ranger is: "I will never leave a fallen comrade to fall into the hands of the enemy." No American was going to be left behind—alive or dead—as far as these soldiers were concerned.

The kidnap operation was in full swing and helicopter support was still desperately needed. With Wolcott's aircraft on the ground, Michael Goffena's Super 62 was alone in providing the "low cap" security for the ground troops who had finished their "precious cargo snatch" and were ready to move.

At this time a fateful decision was made by Air Mission Commander Matthews. He ordered Michael Durant's Super 64 Blackhawk into the action to replace Wolcott in the "low cap" over the insertion area. Durant's mission was to provide suppressive fire against the hundreds of gunmen now massing in the area.

Durant's Blackhawk helicopter, along with three other aircraft, had been in a holding pattern north of the city. Earlier, these aircraft had inserted the Rangers into blocking positions around the target house. These aircraft were on standby in case an emergency extraction became necessary.

The men in these helicopters were tense as they listened to reports of their friends being shot out of the sky. They waited for instructions. They were eager and itching to get back into the fight.

Durant was ready to go. He quickly broke out of the pattern when Lieutenant Colonel Matthews gave him the code word, "Nicole." It was his order to move in. Durant knew that two other Blackhawks had been hit and taken out. Now it was his turn to go into the fury.

No one could know that everyone on that aircraft, except Durant, would soon be dead.

"Durant came down directly in front of me," remembers Michael Goffena, the pilot of the Super 62 Blackhawk for which Durant was now the wingman. "We started a tight little pattern. Almost immediately, I saw Mike's tail rotor get hit."

The other pilots could see small pieces blow away from Durant's aircraft as it went nose low and started losing oil. Immediately Durant's helicopter began smoking. He tried to nurse it back into control and limp away.

"We're hit," was all the other pilots heard Durant say in a very soft voice over the radio.

After Durant's Super 64 had traveled about five hundred meters toward the coast, Michael Goffena could see that Durant wasn't going to make it. He radioed, "Six Four, put it down immediately, you're coming apart."

He no sooner finished these horribly true words than it happened. Goffena watched in horror as Durant's entire tail assembly came apart. The aircraft's nose pitched up and then dipped as the whole tail rotor assembly blew off. Durant's helicopter spun one hundred feet straight in the ground.

The other pilots could hear Durant report on the radio, "We're going in. We're going in hard." Just before the impact, one final transmission was heard when Durant called out to his co-pilot, Ray Frank by saying simply, "Ray."

That was the last anyone heard.

Durant had come down in a field on the outskirts of a densely populated shantytown. When he hit the ground, the aircraft's blades flexed completely off and dirt seemed to explode right back up into the air where the aircraft had been.

Hal Ward, the co-pilot of the fleet's lead aircraft, watched the entire crash and remembers, "It was like slow motion. Mike going in was a sight I'll never forget." Surprisingly, Durant's airframe stayed intact.

Major Ron Cugno, the STAR wing little bird assault commander from Boston, remembers, "When 64 went down, you could almost hear the screams from every cockpit remaining in the sky. We hoped he was going to fly out of it but then he started down. Not only was I frustrated, I was really pissed off."

Goffena, in Super 62, flew over the crash site to look for survivors. "Right away, I knew there were people still alive. I could see both pilots moving in front as well as one of the gunners in the rear of the aircraft," remembers Goffena.

Goffena's door gunner Staff Sergeant Mason Hall saw even more. "I saw Mr. Frank, the left hand pilot, try to get out of his seat, but he couldn't because the seat was so driven down. He was pinned in his aircraft."

Mason Hall also saw his good friend and fellow Crew Chief Tommie Field from Lisbon, Maine, moving in the wreckage. Hall had worked with Tommie for a long time. Almost immediately, Hall's and Field's eyes locked on each other. Then, they waved. Hall knew the wave was a goodbye wave. He was sure Field knew it too. The crowds of people on the ground were approaching the wreckage. Time was running out.

Goffena's Super 62 Blackhawk carried three Special Forces snipers. The snipers were from Fort Bragg's Delta Force. They were specially trained and deadly effective. Two of them, Master Sergeant Gary Gordon, from Lincoln, Nebraska, and Sergeant First Class Randy Shughart from Newville, Pennsylvania, had just received permission to be inserted into Durant's crash site.

Goffena could see a small clearing about fifty meters from the crashed aircraft. As he approached the site, Mason Hall told Gordon they were putting him and Shughart in. Gordon grinned, raised both thumbs, and went to the back of the aircraft with Shughart to prepare for what they knew was a very dangerous mission.

On the first pass of the planned landing site, which was about one hundred meters from Durant's crash site, Goffena could see the area wasn't completely clear. There were scattered shanties throughout the area. One side of the potential landing zone had a roughly built partition with an ox inside.

The Super 62 Blackhawk dropped down and blew the shanty and other debris away to allow a lower drop zone. The snipers, Shughart and Gordon, quickly jumped out of the aircraft from about five feet. Shughart got hung up in some rope and Crew Chief Sergeant Paul Shannon cut him loose. The Delta snipers started in the direction of Durant's crashed helicopter.

Goffena saw that his Special Forces soldiers weren't sure where the crash site was, so a smoke grenade was dropped to mark the spot. By now, Randy Jones and Hal Ward's little bird gunship was in the area. They put down a dense wall of fire, trying desperately to keep the swarming crowds from getting to the injured airmen.

"Almost immediately, we had three RPGs screaming under us," remembers Hal Ward. "It was pretty close to 5 o'clock and just beginning to get dark. We placed an infrared strobe at the crash site so we could see with our NVGs (night vision goggles) later in the night."

Hal Ward also remembers getting low enough to see co-pilot Ray Frank's face. Frank was still trapped in the crashed aircraft. Frank had been in an accident the year before and his expression seemed to say, "I can't believe this shit has happened again."

Ray Frank was a very easy-going and laid-back pilot. He was also Hal Ward's roommate. He had seen and done a lot of highly classified and dangerous operations during his career. But this mission was his most dangerous—and his last.

Hal Ward knew Ray was a dead man when he looked down at his roommate's face for the last time. Then, he spun up and began racing his gunship around the site, trying unsuccessfully to keep the menacing crowds out.

After Super 62 had inserted Shughart and Gordon, they too went into a low racing pattern designed to keep the mob out of the area. They were also desperately trying to keep from being the third Blackhawk shot down that hour.

"We were driving pretty fast over the area," remembers Super 62 Crew Chief Mason Hall. "We were going up and down and juking and jiving, trying to do everything we could not to get hit." The RPG fire was increasing dramatically as the armed Somalis focused on the new crash site.

With Dan Jollota's Search and Rescue aircraft taken out of the action, there was no other backup security "package" for another crash site. Understanding this, Major Ron Cugno, the STAR wing little bird commander asked Air Mission Commander Matthews for permission to drop co-pilots off at the crash site to provide security. His request was denied again and again and finally after his third request denial, he asked no more.

Goffena could see that Shughart and Gordon had reached the crash site. They began getting the injured airmen out of the aircraft to give whatever first aid they could. They also set up a simple security ring concentrating on the main entry from the heavily populated shantytown.

Larry Kulsrud, the wingman for Randy Jones and Hal Ward, in the little bird Barber 52 gunship could see Durant moving. Crew Chief Cleveland had his armor vest off and was being evaluated for wounds by one of the snipers. Ray Frank had been pulled out of the aircraft and was now sitting beside a tree. Someone else rested on his knee, covering the entrance to the densely populated shantytown. Still, another airman could be seen lying on the left side of the aircraft.

The intensity of the ground fire was building fast.

By now, Keith Jones and Karl Maier were also in the area hoping to pull off another extraction of wounded airmen. Jones and Maier had just taken injured men from Wolcott's crash and they wanted desperately to get the injured from Durant's wreckage before it was too late.

They landed at the insertion zone Goffena had used to drop Shughart and Gordon off. Waiting there, they hoped that survivors from the crash site could make it to them for a fast escape.

"I thought there was no way anyone was going to live through this stuff," remembers Keith Jones, the son of a career army man from Texas. "It seemed like we stayed on the ground almost an eternity, but no one came."

Captain Jim Yacone in the STAR wing command aircraft could see that the situation was rapidly deteriorating. He knew that Jones and Maier were sitting targets on the ground. He ordered them out. The last chance for any air rescue was now gone.

Goffena was watching RPGs fly by his aircraft. He shifted into a left hand orbit and started throwing down flash bang grenades. It was getting harder to stay over the top of Durant's crash site and Goffena began to get a very ominous feeling about the situation. He thought, "What is it going to take to end this?" He knew it was only a matter of time and he would be going down too.

Then his left side door gunner got hit.

Crew Chief Paul Shannon was firing his six barrel M-134 minigun at 4,000 rounds per minute when a lucky shot from the ground hit his hand and jammed his gun. Mason Hall slid over to the left side and relieved Shannon. He unjammed the gun and resumed fire. The other Special Forces sniper, Bradley Halling, took over Hall's gun on the right side just as an extremely violent explosion shook the aircraft.

An RPG had just blasted the airship directly under the right door gunner.

All of the windshields were blown out and smoke started filling the shuttering aircraft. Halling, the sniper who had just replaced Mason Hall on the right side gun, had his leg blown off. He was still wide awake, but lying in a puddle of his own blood. The aircraft's co-pilot, Captain Jim Yacone, was knocked out and lying forward on the helicopter's controls.

For a brief instant Mike Goffena was out too.

"I thought we had already hit the ground, but when I came to my senses, I realized we were still in the air," remembers Goffena. "All the warning lights came on. My co-pilot was completely out and leaning on the controls." Responding with automatic reaction developed through countless hours of training, Goffena went into autorotation and leveled the aircraft. He was sure they were on their way into the mobs below them.

"We're going to crash," someone yelled from the back. By now, the radios were jammed with reports of his RPG hit. Goffena had trouble getting on the radio himself but, when he did, he reported to Air Mission Commander Matthews that he would try to make it to New Port.

The blast had blown out his chin bubble and the aircraft's right minigun was knocked out. The left minigun was jammed; without a gunner, it still continued to shoot wildly. The cockpit had turned gray black and Goffena noticed a black sticky material over everything. Later, he realized this sticky stuff was the disintegrated seat cushion from the right door gunner's seat.

The helicopter was leaving a fine trail of smoke. Everything on the control panel was blank. There was nothing wrong with the warning alarms, however, because they kept screaming while Goffena tried to keep his aircraft in the air.

"We went into a deceleration and headed for the road," recalls Goffena. "I realized that a line of power poles were coming up. This really sucked because I didn't think we had a chance of keeping our altitude long enough to get over them."

Goffena kept his aircraft straight and the rotor RPMs held. They barely made it over the wires. The New Port area was coming up. Goffena knew New Port was a secure area.

The helicopter didn't give up. Goffena barely touched the controls as the helicopter went directly in at sixty miles per hour. The explosion had torn off the Blackhawk's right wheel, something Goffena hadn't realized until he landed and promptly veered to the right.

It was dark now. The little bird helicopters were still desperately trying to help Durant and his crew. However, they soon had to be called off. They were needed to help in an even more desperate mission. The ground rescue forces were now being ambushed a short distance away. These were the troops from Fort Drum's 10th Mountain Quick Reaction Force. They were desperately needed to rescue the Task Force Ranger soldiers now fighting their way to Wolcott's Crash Site One.

Shughart, Gordon, and the rest of Durant's crew were never seen alive again. Crew Chief Gordon's mutilated body was dragged through the streets of Mogadishu for the benefit of an admiring world press while a battered Michael Durant was taken prisoner.

However, it would be days before anyone would know what happened during those final minutes.

Michael Durant (far right) along with Bill Cleveland, Tommie Fields, and Ray Frank standing in front of their Super 64 Blackhawk just hours before the action which would leave the crew dead and Durant a prisoner.

The southern crash site two where Sergeants Shughart and Gordon gave their lives to save Michael Durant's life.

The battle scene around the southern crash site two the morning of October 4 showed Malaysian APCs destroyed by Somali RPGs. At the extreme upper right-hand corner of the photo, the crashed helicopter is visible. The soldiers from the 10th Mountain Division fought during the night from the road to the crash site.

Michael Durant being transported on a stretcher after release by his Somali captors.

Michael Durant arriving at the Mogadishu Airport to the thunderous applause of fellow soldiers. He later boarded an aircraft for the flight to a U.S. Army hospital in Germany.

SFC Randall Shughart who gave his life to
save Michael Durant.

SFC Gary Gordon gave his life at the
southern crash site two trying to save the
lives of the crew.

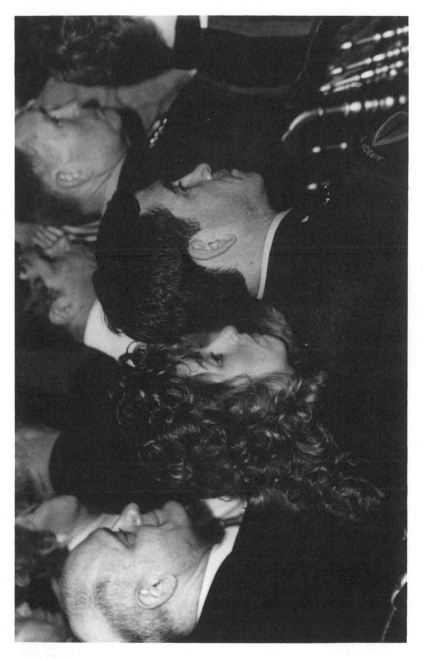

Michael and Lorrie Durant attending the Medal of Honor presentation ceremonies in the White House. Sergeants Shughart and Gordon gave their lives trying to rescue Michael Durant at the southern helicopter crash site. U.S. Army photo.

President Bill Clinton with Stefanie Shughart and Carmen Gordon at the White House ceremony where Randy Shughart and Gary Gordon were given posthumous Medals of Honor. Brittany Gordon is sitting on her mother's lap.

Lt. Larry Perino commanded two of the four blocking positions which secured the initial target building.

Lt. Tom DiTomasso led the first group of Rangers to the first crash site; they were immediately fighting the battle of their lives.

Lt. Col. Dan McKnight, who was the Ranger ground force commander. His splintered band of Rangers were beaten back as they tried to fight their way to crash site one.

SSgt Mark Warner, the fiery Ranger who left the TOC and attempted the first unsuccessful rescue of trapped comrades.

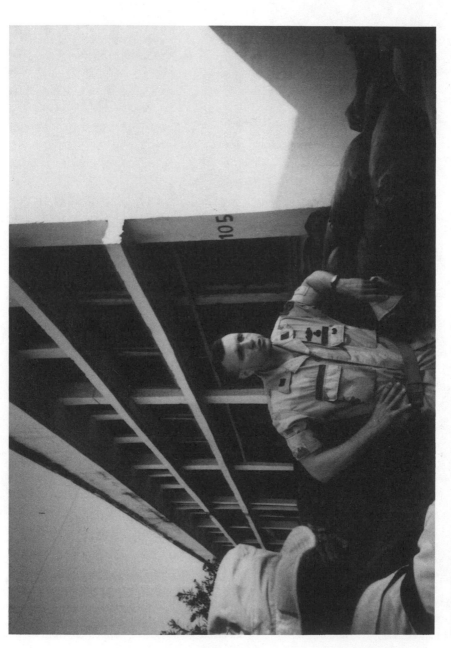

LTC Bill David, who commanded the 10th Mountain Quick Reaction Force which eventually rescued the trapped members of Task Force Ranger.

LTC Dan McKnight and SSgt Mark Warner at the Mogadishu Airport Ranger compound.

During the 18-hour battle there were many individual acts of bravery including those of CW2 Tom Haskell. Shown here next to his Coyote 26 helicopter, Haskell and 1LT Chris Lynch drove into and destroyed a 23-mm antiaircraft gun which had been firing at MH-6 "little birds" at the northern crash site.

10th Mountain Division AH-1F Cobra helicopter in flight over Mogadishu in October 1993.

10th Mountain Cobra helicopter gunships on the flight line of the Mogadishu Airfield looking northeast toward the battle zone.

U.S. Army AH-1F Cobra gunship flying over Mogadishu soon after the October 3 battle.

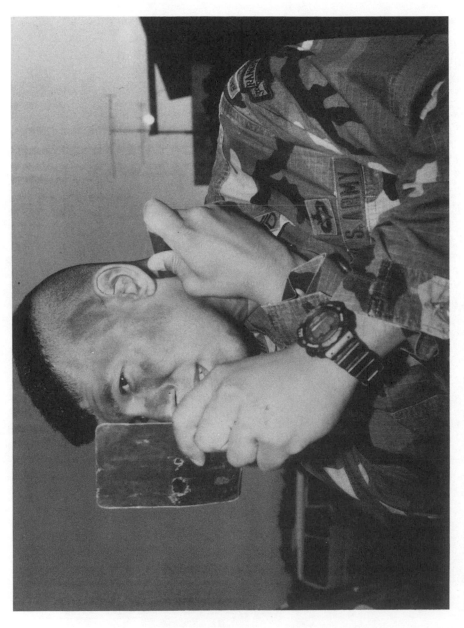

U.S. Army Ranger applying night battle chalk prior to a mission.

Helicopter pilot from the 160th Special Aviation Regiment wearing night-vision goggles which were critical during the night of October 3 to protect the trapped soldiers at crash site one.

Members of the 3rd Ranger Battalion in full battle gear.

Chapter 8

The 2nd Battalion, 14th Infantry Regiment of Fort Drum, New York's 10th Mountain Division, had been in Somalia since July 29. This unit had already seen more action than any other United Nations military group in Somalia.

Many soldiers in this veteran unit had already fought in Desert Storm, Panama, and Grenada. In fact, the 10th Mountain Quick Reaction Force may have seen more close combat battle action than any other active U.S. military Battalion.

Lieutenant Colonel William David from St. Louis, Missouri, a graduate of West Point, was a "no nonsense" 40-year-old commander of this 625-man battalion Task Force. His men were stationed in the University Compound of Mogadishu about three-and-one-half kilometers from the airfield.

On October 3, the battalion's Bravo company was conducting Military Operation Urban Training (MOUT) about three kilometers north of Mogadishu while Charlie company was on Quick Reaction alert. The battalion's Alpha company was serving support and backup during this particular seventy-two-hour cycle. Each of the three companies in the battalion continuously rotated responsibilities.

Each of the three 10th Mountain companies were organized as light infantry units consisting of about 130 men. They were augmented with six five-ton trucks, an antitank platoon, a mobile weapons platoon, and four Humvees with Mark-19 grenade launchers. When a company was serving "quick reaction" duty, they were organized to have a "string" of about two hours which was the time they would need to be on their way from a "cold start" if needed somewhere in the city.

On the Sunday of October 3, Lieutenant Colonel David received notification at 2:15 P.M. that Task Force Ranger had placed a section in the center of Mogadishu off limits. This notification was the first indication to the 10th Mountain headquarters that an operation might occur. Often no further announcement would be given to the headquarters of the 10th Mountain.

At 3:37 P.M. a REDCON ONE alert came from the Task Force Ranger headquarters. That alert instructed David to have his men ready. Immediately, the 10th Mountain commander notified his Quick Reaction Company to "tighten the string" to thirty minutes.

The relative calm of a typical Sunday afternoon was being broken and the studied calm of the battalion's control room was suddenly alive with emotion.

"Oh, shit," were Lieutenant Colonel David's first words when notification of the first downed helicopter came into the headquarters at about 4:10 P.M. Everyone knew they were now "on" for a mission into a part of Mogadishu which was considered the dangerous center of warlord Aidid's territory.

Lieutenant Michael Flaherty, thirty-seven, of Winchester, Massachusetts, recalls the first alerts of October 3. "The first thing I thought about was all the people in the Battalion. They were my friends and we were about to go into harm's way. Naturally, I had concerns for their safety."

At 4:30 P.M., the Quick Reaction Force was summoned to the airport, where they were to serve under the control of Task Force Ranger Commander Major General William Garrison. Lieutenant Colonel David asked the 10th Mountain Aviation Brigade Commander, Colonel Casper, "How urgent is this? Which route should we take to the airport?"

Lieutenant Colonel David needed to know how quickly they were required at the airfield. The company could go a short and direct route which would take them through a dangerous "off limits" area of Mogadishu where four army MPs had recently been killed in an ambush. Or, the company could take a much longer route around the north and western outskirts of the city through a main supply route bypass. This route to the airport would extend the trip significantly.

Quickly, the answer came to Lieutenant Colonel David to go the longer "bypass route." Within minutes the Quick Reaction Force Charlie company, led by their battalion commander, was on the way.

Unfortunately, another word was also quickly spreading, this throughout General Mohammed Aidid's Mogadishu. And that word was that it would only be a matter of time and U.N. pickins around the American crash site would be anything but slim.

It took until 5:24 P.M. for the 10th Mountain column to arrive at the airport via the circuitous bypass route. Traveling a maximum of thirty-five miles an hour on a third world seventeen-kilometer road netted the soldiers only three kilometers from the university compound where they started. By the time they arrived at the airport, new and terrifying information was spreading that a second helicopter had gone down. Lieutenant Colonel David's initial thoughts as he rushed into the Task Force Ranger Tactical Operations Command (TOC) was, "We're in for a big fight."

In the TOC, David saw Major General Garrison, along with Delta Commander Lieutenant Colonel Bill Harold, at the Mogadishu map. There was a lot of activity surrounding them and the radios were all squawking for attention. Quickly, David was given an overview of the situation from the Task Force Ranger commanders. The command knew approximately where the two aircraft had gone down. Word had just arrived that Ranger elements had already secured the first crash site and a fierce battle was going on to hold it. There were also reports of significant casualties.

Lieutenant Colonel David was given instructions to proceed from the airport grounds to secure Michael Durant's Crash Site Two, which, at the time, was under siege with few defenders. The Delta commander pointed to the map and told the 10th Mountain commander, "Bill, we need you to move here quickly to see what we have left."

"Roger, got it," was all David replied. He turned on his heels and stepped outside. With his men again, he planned the mission in his head.

There wasn't much time to discuss military strategy. Lives were at stake and minutes wasted were minutes that could be used by the Aidid forces to marshal their troops into position for deadly ambushes.

A little more than an hour after the 10th Mountain Charlie company arrived, David had shaped it into a combat column. Five-ton trucks and Humvees were moving on their way to what was thought to be the area of Durant's southern crash site. Immediately, the column encountered a series of firefights. These firefights would become a turning point in this battle.

"Our column of vehicles headed north and crossed the K-4 circle," remembers David who rode in an unmarked Humvee about two-thirds of the way back in the string of vehicles. "The lead elements of our column cleared the K-4 circle." The first signs that life was not going to be too pleasant for the next few hours or so became clear to David.

"As my vehicle approached the intersection, I looked left and saw three smoking Humvees crashing toward us," remembers David. "They were traveling lickity split, and it was clear they weren't going to stop."

The soldiers watched the ambush unfold. The early evening air lit up with green and red tracer rounds as the Somalis let go with a torrid attack on the Americans.

"Oh fuck," yelled one of the men in David's vehicle. Lieutenant Colonel David quickly hit his driver's shoulder and yelled, "Fuck Davis, turn here." He pointed to a small crevice between two buildings that might provide some protection.

By now, the front part of the convoy was speeding forward to get out of this predicament while the back third was piling up at the intersection and beginning to return a pretty torrid fire. Before long, the lead elements of the convoy became aware of what was happening behind them. Then they began to receive fire themselves. The convoy stopped. Everyone quickly dismounted their vehicles and sought any cover they could find in alleyways and doorways.

"We had a bit of a mess on our hands," recalls Lieutenant Colonel David. "It was pretty apparent to me that we were going to have to mount a completely different kind of effort if we were ever going to make it into the objective area."

By now, everyone in the Task Force Ranger TOC was aware of the problem. Tenth Mountain Commander Brigadier General Greg Gile was in country for a "change of command" ceremony and from the TOC he radioed Lieutenant Colonel David, "Regroup your forces and return to the airport immediately."

David simply replied, "Roger," and quickly was on the radio to his Charlie company commander, Captain Mike Whetstone. "Break contact and move elements back to this position. Meet me south of K-4 and we'll do a headcount there."

First Sergeant Gary Doody, a native of Kentwood, Michigan, had always been one of the coolest members of the entire company under fire. During the next half hour of hell, he and his men repeatedly gave the Somalis more than they would have liked. Just the week before he had been involved in an action where he saw one of his company gunners get shot. Reacting quickly, he ran directly into enemy fire to drag his wounded comrade back to safety. This action would eventually be acknowledged with a Silver Star.

His second medal action was about to occur.

"The ambush we were in the week before was kind of like a scrimmage for the one we got into on Sunday night," says Doody. "I can't believe anybody was really surprised about what we were going through. We all pretty much knew it was going to be a hell of a fight as we entered the area."

An avid deer hunter in Michigan, Doody knew more than a little about baiting traps for unsuspecting animals during deer season. But the Somalis were now the hunters. And they used their minutes well as they prepared a deadly reception for their American rescuers who they well knew were on the way to the helicopter crash sites.

But being forewarned is not necessarily being forearmed. The only transport the American troops rushing to the rescue were the Humvees and open-top five-ton trucks. The trucks had sandbags mounted on the sides which might stop a bullet or two. Otherwise, these vehicles offered scant protection from the seemingly limitless arsenal of terror enjoyed by the Aidid forces.

"What was unique about this ambush was that the Somalis were all over the tops of the buildings," says Doody. "During a normal ambush you could take cover; here, the Somalis commanded the 'high ground.' We took fire from every direction."

After the front elements of the ambushed column received their orders from Lieutenant Colonel David to turn back, Doody remembers a conversation he had with Charlie company commander, Captain Michael Whetstone from Alexandria, Virginia.

"Hey Sir, I think we are in a hell of a bind," said Doody almost lightly.

"Yes, I guess you're right Sergeant. O.K., let's try and get the trucks turned around. I'll keep a line of fire to protect you," replied the calmly thinking Whetstone.

The crackling sounds of bullets came from every direction and RPGs were flying everywhere as the lead elements of the convoy began their fight into the ambush area. "Your first concern is to make sure everyone stays as safe as possible," remembers Captain Whetstone. "Sometimes, even what seems to be failure can serve a purpose for a group of men tasting the horrors of war. This retreat was our wake-up call. There is no question we made the right choice to go back and prepare another assault."

While this was happening, Major General Montgomery back at the airport command center was on the command net directing Malaysian and Pakistani armored units to begin movement to the New Port area where they were to prepare for another rescue mission. This multinational group had the only armored vehicles in the city and these vehicles were going to be desperately needed to push through the ever tightening Somali death ring.

For Physician's Assistant Lieutenant Michael Flaherty, who was riding in one of the lead trucks of the ambushed convoy, braving Somali fire was not a time for deep thinking. "What was going on in my head was my job. This whole thing was incredibly frightening because we had Somali fire coming from everywhere and I had people getting wounded all around me."

Flaherty's pride in the actions of his comrades grew as he saw the men of his company leap from their trucks to get a better line of fire into the Somali positions. To do so, the vehicles made a U-turn, and unfortunately ended up on the opposite side of the four-lane road trying to find cover from the increasing RPG fire. After the Americans made their U-turn, the Somalis realized the troops who had dismounted from the vehicles would have to cross the street in the open to get back to their trucks.

This was the opportunity they wanted.

"You know, I consider myself something of an amateur historian," says Flaherty, who stayed with the wounded men who couldn't get out of the trucks. "And I happen to think what I watched next had to be one of the most courageous things I have ever seen. Those guys selflessly risked their lives to protect each other as they raced across that street. And then Sergeant Doody went back into the street, completely unprotected, to save the life of a wounded soldier."

Sergeant Doody remembers, "We were all crunched down on one side of the street, shooting up at the buildings. We knew we had to get across the street to our trucks, which were now wedged between some buildings to avoid RPG fire."

Of course, when a soldier is running across a street they aren't firing their weapons too accurately. Therefore, only a few would cross at a time. The others stayed behind to cover the dangerous sprints.

The Somalis waited for their "turkey shoot."

The 10th Mountain company had practiced these "run for your life" drills before. Now they were about to do it for real.

The men broke into the open. A fire team stayed behind to provide fire cover while the rest of the platoon broke across the road. The men that crossed then provided covering fire for the others to cross.

The process worked fine. But, when both teams had crossed the road, they looked back. They watched with horror as a wounded man on his hands and knees tried to crawl to safety.

It was Sergeant Carroll. He had a chest and shoulder wound.

"Try to get me some cover because I'm going to get this guy," Sergeant Doody shouted to Sergeant Watson beside him. The fire was now so intense from both the Somali and American positions, it was a miracle that Carroll was still alive.

Doody figured now was as good a time as any. Without much thought he made a one hundred-meter dash that was as memorable as any he may have made on his Michigan high school track team. He quickly linked up with his wounded comrade.

"Hey, you all right?" shouted Doody over the fire.

"I've been shot," was the frightened reply as the soldier pointed to his bloody shoulder and chest.

"Do you think you can make it across the street with me?"

"I think I can," was the reply. Doody said, "Well O.K., then let's haul ass and get out of here."

With his good arm around Doody's shoulder, Carroll began to run as best he could. For the most part, however, he was dragged by his rescuer across the street. The other soldiers could hardly believe these men weren't shot. When Doody and Carroll reached the truck side of the street, they were quickly placed in the back of a truck that immediately sped away.

The entire convoy started racing down the street toward the K-4 circle. Most of the soldiers ran beside their vehicles, firing their weapons. The tactic gave them better mobility and better accuracy.

By now, the American soldiers were running low on ammunition. "Take it easy on your fire because we're running low on the stuff," Doody started yelling to his men. Each man was down to about fifty rounds of ammo from their original five hundred rounds. And they were facing the same deadly route back to the airfield from which they had just come.

Minutes later, PFC Eugene Pamer felt something hit him in the back. He knew he was hit. The bullet went right through his flak jacket. Sergeant Richard Knight noticed him bleeding "like a stuck pig," but the young private wouldn't stop fighting. As the company maneuvered their way back over the K-4 traffic circle, Pamer went down on his stomach, spraying machine-gun fire to cover his comrades as they ran across the intersection.

"And then he picked up his weapon and kept going," remembers Captain Whetstone. "He was bleeding and obviously hurt, but he was thinking first about the safety of his buddies." Machine gunners are usually the first target the enemy seeks to destroy because they are obvious and very destructive.

Pamer was noticed, but he wasn't killed. He would receive a Silver Star for his actions.

The American convoy finally took what seemed like an eternity as they crossed into the American zone south of the K-4 circle. Arriving back at the airfield about 7 P.M., Lieutenant Colonel David quickly reported to General Gile in the TOC.

The General had a grim face. The sound of combat could be clearly heard over the radios in the TOC. This was not a place for small talk and a very calm and reassuring General Gile told the colonel of the new plan which involved two Malaysian APC companies and a Pakistani tank platoon.

David remained silent, but the significance of unspoken words echoed in his head, "What the fuck am I going to do with these guys?"

He would soon find out.

Chapter 9

Michael Durant from Berlin, New Hampshire, knew his aircraft was hit and going down. He just didn't know whether he could keep the aircraft up long enough to get out of the battle area before the Blackhawk went down. He put the aircraft's nose down and started out of there.

He couldn't have known then, but the married thirty-two-year-old pilot and father of a one-year-old boy had spent virtually his entire adult life preparing for the next eleven days.

Signing up for the army in 1979 just barely out of high school, Durant knew he wanted to fly helicopters since he was fourteen. He became a warrant officer and a helicopter pilot four years later. In 1987, he was accepted to fly for the army's most elite helicopter service, the 160th Special Operations Aviation Regiment, otherwise known as the "Night Stalkers."

One of his first opportunities to test himself came in 1988 with the army's nineteen-day Survival, Evasion, Resistance and Escape training conducted at the U.S. Army John F. Kennedy Special Warfare Center and School at Fort Bragg, North Carolina. Trainees in this class endure almost inhumane physical tests, including sleep deprivation, starvation diets, and a series of personality challenges aimed at helping them survive whatever fates warfare might throw at them.

Soldiers completing this training emerge as "McGyver-like" figures able to go it alone on a mission for months after having developed abilities to gather food, evade capture, and perform technical tasks needed for survival such as hooking up a radio from very basic parts.

This training was important because it allowed him to withstand the rigors of the next eleven days. He was blindfolded and handcuffed, and he suffered from injuries sustained in the crash and from a gunshot wound to his left arm.

Somalia was not the first real-life test of Durant's warrior skills. A helicopter pilot in the Panama invasion in 1989 and during the Gulf War a little over a year later, Durant was awarded a Distinguished Flying Cross and two Air Medals for his actions in the cockpit.

But when the call came in August 1993 for the young father to pack up for yet another exotic locale, Durant was less than enthusiastic. "To be honest, I didn't want to go," remembers Durant. There may be nothing better than a miniature version of your own flesh and blood crawling around on the living room carpet to adjust your priorities.

Despite whatever personal misgivings Durant may have had, he needed only fifteen minutes to prepare for his journey. "I remember seeing the trees along the road as we headed out," remembers Durant. "I wondered if I would ever see them again." He was on his way to the assignment which would change his life. He could never realize then what lay ahead and the kind of fame his actions would bring.

The first few weeks of Durant's mission in Somalia were a tense waiting game. No one knew when the call might come that the elusive Aidid had been spotted. After being called in on the Task Force's seventh mission that fateful October 3 as the replacement for Wolcott's downed Super 61 chopper, Durant did his best to ring the area with fire. After only four or five circles, his aircraft's tail rotor was hit by a rocket-propelled grenade and like the veteran pilot he was, he lowered his nose and started out of the area.

"It felt like a speed bump when we got hit," remembers Durant. "The aircraft flew pretty normally after the hit and I headed out of there."

He didn't get far. About a mile south of the target building, Durant could feel his aircraft pitch up and then drop like a rock. His tail assembly had completed disintegration started by the RPG.

"We dropped from about a hundred feet," says Durant. "The aircraft began spinning and the horizon became a blur. This is pretty terrifying." Durant struggled to keep the aircraft upright because he realized that if the Blackhawk could land on its wheels, the crash would be cushioned. Maybe they would survive.

The crash was a slow motion explosion, but the helicopter did hit with its wheels first.

When Durant regained consciousness a few minutes later, he was confused, his back hurt like he couldn't believe, and a bloody white piece of broken bone was protruding from his right thigh. He could see debris spread throughout the cockpit. He couldn't move.

The aircraft had gone down about a mile south of the first crash site in a residential area which was not yet part of the action. In fact, witnesses reported later that people initially ran away from the crashed helicopter. But, there was no mistaking this fact—the Somalia militia were on their way.

"Are you OK?" Durant asked looking to his left at co-pilot Ray Frank. There was only a short nod. Frank said his back hurt as he struggled to get out of his seat.

Durant could hear one of his crew chiefs, Bill Cleveland, directly behind him, starting to talk. It was clear he was severely injured as was the other crew chief, Tommie Fields, who was also beginning to move. Durant was relieved that everyone was alive.

Almost immediately, there was the sound of other helicopters circling overhead. He wasn't sure who these aircraft belonged to or what was going to happen next. He did know that he wasn't able to get out of his seat.

Before long, Fort Bragg, North Carolina, Special Forces snipers Master Sergeant Gary Gordon and Sergeant First Class Randall Shughart were at his broken cockpit window. Durant did not know how they got there, but it felt good to have them around. Maybe he and his men would get out of this mess after all.

Randy Shughart, from southeastern Pennsylvania, was a leader who enjoyed the simple pleasures of military life. He was so committed to his career in Special Forces that he made his wife promise him before they got married that she would never ask him to leave the military. Maine native Gary Gordon also loved the life of the Green Beret "silent professional." He had two small children back home in North Carolina, but right now all he was thinking about was his job and saving the lives of the helicopter crewmen.

"I explained my injuries and they gently lifted me up," Durant remembers. "Those guys were obviously concerned for my well-being." Shughart and Gordon raised Durant from his seat and placed him about fifteen feet to the right of the crashed aircraft and then began helping the other injured men. Sergeant Bill Cleveland was placed next to a tree about ten feet to Durant's left. He was face down. One of the snipers placed a weapon in Durant's lap.

It was not long before armed Somalis began to arrive. Durant started firing his weapon from the right side. He could hear Gordon and Shughart firing on the left. "Those guys placed me in the perfect position," says Durant. "There were only two ways anyone could come into our area and I had a perfect view of both. I was able to control the whole right side of the aircraft while they were firing their weapons from the left." Durant only had two magazines of ammunition. He knew they would soon be gone.

And then Durant heard what he feared most.

Shughart had a unique and distinct voice. In the confusion of the intense Somali attack, Durant heard that voice scream, "I'm hit. I'm hit." Shughart went down.

"I was nearly out of ammo," remembers Durant. He slowed his fire in order to save what little ammunition he had left. Then, for no apparent reason, the Somali guns became silent.

Gordon ran over and asked Durant if there were any other weapons in the crashed helicopter. Durant told him there was another M-16. Gordon handed Durant a CAR-15, which is a variation of the fully automatic M-16 rifle. This was Shughart's weapon. Durant knew Shughart must be dead.

Gordon retrieved the other M-16 from the aircraft. Then Durant heard him call on the survival radio. He gave a quick and grim situation report. The aircraft that landed the Special Forces snipers had already been hit and was now limping back to base. Durant could hear someone tell Gordon that a ground reaction force was "en route." Gordon must have known, as Durant did, that they would never get there in time.

Gordon looked back at Durant with a slight smile and said, "Time to get some more Somalis," and he ran to the left side of the aircraft as the regrouped Somalis started their final attack. This was the last time Durant saw Gordon.

"I continued to shoot on my side until I ran out of ammo," remembers Durant. "A grenade landed next to me and I was able to knock it away before it exploded." The Somalis were now mounting a coordinated and consolidated attack on the left side of the crashed aircraft. Durant knew it was only a matter of time. Gordon couldn't hold on much longer. The end was near.

"I could hear a huge volume of fire starting from the left side of the aircraft." Durant knew the Somalis were going directly at Gordon, the only American still able to fight. Durant heard Gordon cry out. Then there was a terrifying instant of silence.

"The most terrifying sound I ever heard was when the firing stopped and the mob appeared," recalls Durant. Within seconds a crazed mob overran the site. "I was sure they were going to kill me as I was sure they were killing everyone else."

Durant put his hands up in the air and looked at the sky. He became as passive as possible. It was out of his hands now.

The mob began to attack Durant. Half of the people began to beat him while the other half fought each other to see who would get his clothes and his equipment. Someone in the crowd must have realized that an American pilot was worth more alive than dead because Durant could see one of the Somalis trying to keep the others away.

Durant's potential killers were barely warded off as others began to protect him. Eventually, the severely injured pilot was pulled out of the area in excruciating pain with an open fracture and a crushed back vertebrae.

"They had taken off my clothes and they continued to beat me," remembers Durant. "They started parading me around in the streets naked." One Somali threw dirt in Durant's eyes and mouth, then wrapped a rag around his head. Others hoisted him over their shoulders and began dragging him through the streets of Mogadishu. Still other Somalis began beating his head and face with canes and clubs.

Durant was taken to a small house and thrown into a dirty, dark room. He was chained into a corner. His leg was much more severely deformed and the pain was excruciating.

Durant could at times hear confusion outside his door. Once he heard someone walk to the door and open it slightly. Then, in an instant, a rifle barrel appeared. The rifle fired one shot, striking him in the left arm. Later, he was told that the crowd outside the house wanted to come in and kill him. Durant knew that he would have to call on all the reserves of courage his fourteen years of military training had instilled in him to survive.

The first couple of days in captivity were the hardest. Durant was terrified. The constant thought that he might never see his wife and child again was more painful than his wounds.

Durant began secretly working to free his hands. They had been tied behind his back with what were becoming razor-sharp cords. Finally, he freed one hand and then another, all the while not letting his captors know of his success. "That was a big victory for me," says Durant. "I could now wipe the dirt out of my eyes and move my legs around." After each moment of freedom from his cords, he dutifully tied himself back up so his guards wouldn't realize he was actually free of his bonds.

On his second day of captivity, Durant was forced to make a video which aroused the anger of the world. He was able to withstand this test with honor by giving textbook answers, so as to provide only the vaguest of intelligence, information that would not endanger his comrades. "When you're watching John Wayne movies, you think all you need to do is give your name, rank, and serial number," says Durant. "But, if you take a hard line like that, all you do is make it hard on yourself."

The video had another effect. Durant's wife, Lorrie, now knew that her husband had somehow survived the firestorm which was making headlines around the world.

On the second day in captivity, a doctor came into his room. He had 4x4 bandages and Betadine to clean Durant's open leg wound. He was also given antibiotics and aspirin. Over the next few days, he was moved twice as it became clear that Aidid and his top lieutenants now considered Durant a political tool.

Durant stopped seeing guards carrying guns. He was also given a bath before Red Cross officials came to see him for the first time on October 8, five days after his capture. One afternoon he was asked what he would like to eat. He answered spaghetti. "I kind of thought that something like filet mignon was not one of my choices," says Durant. "But the spaghetti was actually quite good. It helped keep me going."

Although most of Durant's guards would have just as soon killed him as look at him, others guarding Durant were actually kind and tried to comfort him. He was told, "If Allah wills it, you will go home."

"I guess a human being is a human being, no matter what nationality they are," says Durant.

Communicating with his Italian-speaking captors was a haphazard affair. But he managed to use his knowledge of Spanish to get across basic concepts of pain and hunger. He had been given a radio by now and he listened to the Armed Forces Network play the first song on each hour in his honor. "That helped me tremendously," recalls Durant.

Back in Tennessee, Lorrie kept the home fires burning.

On the day of the failed mission, she had heard about the crash of two Blackhawk helicopters. She was prepared for the worst and was ready for the arrival of the two uniformed men in her driveway to give her the bad news. But a call from a friend a few hours later that her husband had just appeared on CNN sent a wave of joy and hope through the twenty-seven-year-old homemaker. Without cable television in her own home, Lorrie's television had been used to play a *Beauty and the Beast* tape to keep her toddler Joey amused.

Life for the Durant family had to go on. When it came time for Mike's sister's wedding during the Saturday of his captivity, there was no thought of calling it off. The only switch in plans was the national news coverage the event garnered.

Back in Mogadishu, Aidid's Minister of Internal Affairs began visiting Durant on a daily basis. The purpose of this visit was obviously to report Durant's status to Aidid. "He came each day and explained what was going on," remembers Durant. "One day he came in and told me I was going home within forty-eight hours."

Durant did not want to get his hopes up. But, when the Minister came back the next day, he told the pilot that he would be released after Aidid's press conference the next day. A few hours later, a Nigerian soldier who had also been a prisoner was brought into Durant's room. He had been told he would be released also.

The next twenty-four hours were filled with hope and fear for Durant. After his helicopter crashed, after his crew and the two brave Special Forces snipers were killed at his crash site, after his capture when there were times he was sure he would die, and now after eleven days in captivity, would he really go home? Would he actually see his wife and child again?

It didn't seem possible.

But it was becoming apparent that Somalian warlords did not have the stomach of Iranian mullahs. The hunted Aidid had decided that the release of Durant and the Nigerian U.N. Peacekeeper would help his cause. International goodwill was more important than holding these men longer, or even killing them.

At 11 A.M. the next day, Aidid had a press conference in which he announced the prisoners' release. At 12:30 P.M., Red Cross workers took possession of the soldiers. Durant was going home. He had no idea to what.

He had the attention of the world's media. His battered face was pictured on the covers of *Time, Newsweek*, and *U.S. News & World Report*. He could not possibly have known how famous he had become.

But there was one thing he did know. And that was the gratitude he felt toward the two men who had given their lives for him eleven days earlier. Unfortunately, he would never be able to thank Gary Gordon and Randy Shughart.

Chapter 10

Lieutenant Colonel William David, the Task Force commander of the 2–14 Infantry, had just been given the assignment of his life. His orders were to assemble a rescue operation made up of three nations, and do it quickly. Rangers were dying at Crash Site One and no one knew what had happened at Crash Site Two.

And while he knew there was not much possibility of survivors at the second crash, there might be bodies to be recovered and valuable equipment to be destroyed before it fell into enemy hands. The forty-year-old commander knew there was a lot riding on his shoulders.

Lieutenant Colonel David's initial recoil at the prospect of hastily organizing foreign troops fighting under the United Nations command stemmed from logistical horrors dancing in his head.

"It was going to be a very complicated mission," recalls David. "We were not even sure these foreign troops spoke our language much less had the same fire control measures and radio frequencies we did."

While some of his fears were well-founded, in the end what determined mission outcome was just plain commonsense soldiering. In fact, Lieutenant Colonel David was about to learn that when time and survival is at stake, nations with different languages, backgrounds, and traditions can join forces and accomplish a mission.

The plan was starting to gel. The primary effort would be to extract the Rangers at the Wolcott Crash Site One and then send another contingent of rescue soldiers to the southern Crash Site Two. "By about 2030 (8:30 P.M.), I felt we had enough combat power to get rolling," recalls David.

The rescue plan included air support. The multinational teams would be aided from the skies by the 10th Mountain's 2–25 "Raven" attack helicopter company commanded by Lieutenant Colonel Robert Lee Gore from Georgia. His pilots were well aware of the situation and were itching to join in the fray. "Our Cobra helicopter gunships had been here since June," recalls Raven pilot Jim Neely. "We knew the Somalis feared us. We also knew their fears were justified."

Task Force Ranger Liaison Major Craig Nixon began work as well. He quickly put together a composite platoon of Rangers that included guards, cooks, and mechanics to help with the rescue.

By about 7:20 P.M., the Ranger Company at the northern crash site reported they had established a defensive perimeter and were waiting for the rescue force. "They were pinned down," says Lieutenant Colonel David. "Both they knew and we knew they wouldn't be able to get out of there alone."

While Lieutenant Colonel David was microplanning each detail of the increasingly complex plan, precious minutes were ticking away, minutes he knew could mean the difference for the surrounded Rangers with their severely wounded.

Just in case he needed one, Lieutenant Colonel David recalls a Task Force Ranger member who began acting as his own personal "cattle prod."

"Those helicopters have been down for five hours now," the Ranger began reminding the commander. "We have a pilot who is hurt."

Unfortunately, the planning for the rescue force could not move any faster.

Some of the troops preparing to go out had just returned from the Quick Reaction Force's first failed rescue attempt. These men had learned that Somali ambushes occur in the most unforgiving conditions of Mogadishu's urban slums. These men knew that every window and doorway could conceal an enemy sniper. And many times they did.

"It was kind of like 'Oh Fuck'," recalls 10th Mountain Sergeant Richard Knight. "I could still see the look on the faces of those Somalis shooting at us the hour before. I mean, I almost got blown away. I had just survived an ambush and I wanted some time to think."

When the rescue troops began moving, the plan was for them to meet with the multinational force at New Port less than a kilometer east of the airfield. The multinational force consisting of Malaysians and Pakistanis would supply the needed armored vehicles and tanks absolutely necessary for the mission's success.

Unfortunately, Secretary of Defense Les Aspin had turned down desperate requests from the American commanders in the field for U.S. armored vehicles the month before. Despite repeated appeals for these vehicles, which could have easily and quickly ended this whole nightmare, Aspin was convinced that politically, American armored vehicles would send the wrong message to the Somalis. He therefore repeatedly denied these requests from his field commanders and even from General Colin Powell, the chairman of the Joint Chiefs of Staff.

As a result of the secretary's fateful decision, desperate hours were lost as arrangements continued to be made with other United Nation's forces to use their vehicles. It was during these precious moments that Corporal James Smith lay bleeding to death in a slum shanty at Crash Site One. The necessary armored rescue force was not yet possible.

A plan continued to be formed. From New Port, the entire rescue force would head north toward National Street. The convoy would be headed by two Pakistani tanks to clear the way. The contingent would boldly ram into enemy territory in the hope of scaring off any more ambushes with this show of determined force.

Once on National Street, the multinational task force, consisting of over one hundred vehicles, would break up. Alpha company would continue on to the northern crash site with the Malaysian armored personnel carriers to rescue the trapped soldiers there. Charlie company would break off and proceed directly to the southern crash site.

As the men started moving out of the airport grounds toward New Port for the multinational link up, the Third platoon leader of Quick Reaction Force's Charlie company remembers, "There were those who really kept their cool while others started saying 'Man, I can't really believe I got to go back through this stuff again'."

Arriving at New Port, Lieutenant Colonel David began the coordination between his two companies, the composite Ranger platoon, four aging U.S. built M-48 Paki tanks with their Pakistani crews, and the thirty-two Malaysian armored personnel carriers (APCs). The Malaysian commanders quickly agreed to allow Americans to replace the Malaysian troops in these vehicles, but the drivers still had to be Malaysian.

These Malaysian personnel carriers were German-made Condor vehicles described by one American soldier as a "floating casket on wheels." The vehicles had a driver up front and a porthole in the back for a machine gunner. Each vehicle could hold about six troops.

"When we arrived at New Port, it was dark," remembers Lieutenant Colonel David. "We had our work cut out for us because we had to communicate and coordinate our plans quickly with the Malaysian and Pakistani commanders. We had never worked with these people before."

The potential Tower of Babel at New Port was alleviated somewhat by the fact that many of the Malaysians managed a passable pidgin English. However, with American, Pakistani, and Malaysian vehicles all lined up at the sprawling complex and with almost three hundred soldiers trying to quickly get organized for the mission, it was anything but smooth sailing.

"What the hell is going on here?" recalls Lieutenant Colonel David being asked more than once. "Where do we go?" asked others.

New Port was the Pakistani area of responsibility. Knowing the area better than the Americans, Pakistani officials made a recommendation for a route change to the crash site which David quickly agreed to. The Malaysians were amenable to whatever plan would be decided and stayed in the background during the plan-making negotiations.

Americans trying to get into the Malaysian APCs found opening the doors of these strange-looking vehicles to be one of the most challenging hurdles at New Port. After some gesturing with the Malaysian drivers and then some "not so gentle" encouragement of the doors, the Americans were able to board what they hoped would be relatively safe cocoons.

Some of these soldiers were disabused of the notion of invulnerability as the RPGs started flying a few minutes later.

By 10:40 P.M., the column was finally ready to head out with the Pakistani tanks in the lead to plow through any ambush-enticing obstacles the Somalis had placed in their path. In fact, the wrecked hulks of automobiles were frequently thrown in the road by enemy forces hoping to snare American prey by getting them to step from their vehicles to remove them.

"The threat to the tanks was not great," recalls David. "The tanks would handle the road obstacles. And tanks are scary to foot soldiers."

The convoy's air cover would be courtesy of the 10th Mountain's Task Force Raven helicopters. These air warriors were ready to go and they already had a scouting OH-58d Warrior helicopter night scanning the roads ahead for enemy troops.

The Raven helicopters would accompany the column throughout most of the trip to a prearranged point on National Street where the 160th Special Aviation MH-6 little bird gunships would take over protection of the ground contingent heading to the northern Crash Site One. National Street would then become an aerial boundary with the 10th Mountain Ravens continuing to cover the south and the 160th Special Aviation Regiment little birds covering the north.

And then trouble hit. This time it wasn't in the form of Somali firepower.

"Colonel, I have been instructed by my brigade commander that he doesn't want us to take the lead," said the Paki tank commander.

"What the fuck, do you mean?" replied David with a not so diplomatic inflection in his voice.

"I'm sorry but my brigade commander has instructed me not to take the lead," repeated the Pakistani.

Lieutenant Colonel David collected his thoughts for a moment realizing how tenuous this whole multinational operation was. He tried to make the best of the situation. "Well, where can your tanks move?"

"We can go toward the front of the column, but not to the front," was the reply.

Quickly, before the rest of the column started having troops leave their vehicles and before other vehicles started leaving the formation, David worked out a gentleman's agreement. The Pakistanis would lead the column out of the New Port area because they were the only ones who knew the previously agreed-to route. At a traffic circle where the convoy was going to turn left onto National Street, the front two lead tanks would drop back and become the third and fourth vehicles, thereby following the wishes of the Pakistani commanders.

David knew that the Pakistani captain was breaking orders from his colonel with this compromise. He expressed his appreciation with a handshake.

With this change in plans, more precious time was spent relaying the information to drivers and company commanders.

By 23:30 (11:30 P.M.), the column finally began moving out with a plan solidly understood at the company commander level, vaguely grasped at the platoon leader level, and absolutely unclearly understood at the individual soldier's level.

The Americans at the northern Crash Site One had now been under siege for nearly seven hours. No one knew what had happened at the southern Crash Site Two. But everyone suspected the worse. The Quick Reaction Force was finally under way for the last rescue attempt.

Chapter 11

The multinational rescue force left New Port at 11:30 P.M. The 106-vehicle convoy under the command of Lieutenant Colonel William David headed north and east to National Street where they would turn left and head west, directly into Mohammed Aidid's killing fields.

At the prearranged traffic circle, the two lead Pakistani tanks dropped back and became the third and fourth vehicles in the convoy. The lead was now taken over by two Malaysian APCs carrying Quick Reaction Force Alpha company troops in the back.

"Almost immediately as we turned onto National Street, we started receiving a rain of automatic weapons and RPG fire," remembers David. "We started fighting our way literally one building and one block at a time."

Illumination flares began appearing in the sky. The flares blinded helicopter pilots and convoy drivers who wore infrared night-vision goggles.

"Who's firing the flares?" yelled out David. "Stop all flares! Stop all flares!" was the immediate radio order given throughout the convoy. It soon became clear, however, that the United Nations forces weren't shooting the flares. The Somalis were marking their own mortar coordinates. And they were using flares to do it.

By midnight, the troops had fought their way to a small intersection on National Street. This intersection was checkpoint Charlie, where the plan called for part of the convoy to proceed north to the first crash site while another part would go south to Durant's crash site. It was here that the lead Malaysian APC driver made the most costly mistake of his life.

Arriving at the intersection, the two lead APCs, driven by the Malaysians carrying an Alpha company platoon, were supposed to head north to the Wolcott crash site. Instead, in the confusion, the APCs turned south toward the Durant site. "It's the old story of a plan made in haste. Those drivers may not have known they were supposed to go north," says David.

Stuck in the second APC was the second platoon leader of Alpha company, Lieutenant Mark Hollis. Not able to communicate with their driver, the American Quick Reaction Force soldiers in the first two APCs weren't sure where they were, but assumed that their drivers did.

But even knowing the route would not have done much good for Hollis. He was stuck inside the APC and was unable to see where he was going. It was up to the Malays, who were forced into the convoy's lead position to blaze a trail in a section of the city they were not familiar with. "We could feel our driver slow down and then just bolt ahead. I guess the driver of the APC behind us didn't want to leave his buddy, so he followed," remembers Hollis.

About 1,000 meters into their mistaken and misguided route, disaster struck in the form of two perfectly pitched RPGs. The first one took out the lead vehicle. The Malaysian driver suffered wounds that would prove fatal later that night. The other RPG hit the engine of the second vehicle, which was now smoking.

A terrifying silence overtook the soldiers in the second vehicle. Lieutenant Hollis wondered what to do. He stuck his head out the door and realized the first vehicle was destroyed and that they were in the middle of a "fuckin' kill zone." "In this kind of situation," says Hollis, "soldiers are taught to get the hell out of there."

But, the lieutenant soon realized that not only was he in a kill zone, he was all alone in the kill zone. There were no vehicles behind him, only a burning one in front. Bullets were flying everywhere. More than a few slammed into his vehicle.

"Holy Shit," he exclaimed, as he began to experience the worst feeling he ever had. He quickly dropped back into his vehicle to brief his soldiers on their ominous situation.

A new plan was devised quickly, one that was formed by the light of a high-tech horror show where tracers from all the firepower directed against them created a scene straight out of *Star Wars*.

The Lieutenant knew their only hope was to leave the vehicle and set up a security perimeter. The surviving soldiers in the first vehicle needed to be tended to. And they had to establish communication with the rest of the convoy.

Fortunately, the soldiers were next to a walled compound. Hollis thought the wall might offer his men some protection. "Can you put a hole in that wall?" asked Lieutenant Hollis of his engineer.

"Roger, sir," was the quick reply.

A seven-pound plastic satchel charge was placed at the base of the wall and detonated without delay. The blast was way too big for the wall. The whole wall blew down. "Fortunately, I had my NOD goggles on; otherwise I would have had a broken nose out of that blast," says Lieutenant Hollis.

While the Americans quickly dashed behind the newly formed rubble into a courtyard, the Malaysian APC crews remained inside their damaged vehicles. The Malays decided to stay there. Their decision only served to make their vehicles even more inviting targets for the seemingly limitless supply of RPGs the Somalis had to offer. "I think they thought they were invulnerable inside those vehicles even though one was still smoking," remembers Lieutenant Hollis. "There was nothing we could do to convince them to come with us."

The front APC got hit again.

The driver of the Malaysian APC was already critically wounded from the first RPG blast. After the second blast, he crawled from his vehicle. The Americans could see large chunks of his face were missing. He started crawling toward the wall rubble the Americans were hiding behind gurgling a gruesome, "Help me. Help me."

Some of the soldiers ran out to him and helped him to safety. A medic tried to patch him up. It was clear he wasn't going to live much longer.

Behind the wall, an M-60 gunner tried to respond to the firestorm raging on the street. But it was a herculean task. Every round of his M-60 fire seemed to invite more and more RPG fire.

Lieutenant Hollis attempted to contact his Alpha company commander, Captain Drew Meyerowich, who was now fighting his way north to the Wolcott crash site. Unsuccessful, he tried to contact Lieutenant Colonel David who had set up a command post at the intersection on National Street. Lieutenant Colonel David knew that Lieutenant Hollis's two APCs had gone on alone, but there were no spare troops he could send to find them. Everyone was fighting for their lives in the darkness of this fierce battle.

"Dragon Six. This is Terminator 26," Lieutenant Hollis called out on the radio to the convoy commander, Lieutenant Colonel David. "Dragon Six. This is Terminator 26. Please come in."

"Hey son, you're alive," Lieutenant Colonel David said when he heard his Lieutenant. "What's your situation?"

Lieutenant Hollis quickly painted the grim picture of his platoon pinned down and without vehicles. "We've got a bit of a shit sandwich down here sir, and we are taking a huge bite."

"Roger Terminator 26. I understand the situation. Just keep doing what you are doing and we'll get some help your way as soon as we can." Lieutenant

Colonel David wasn't sure when that would be. All of his forces were now engaged. He continued, "Helicopter gunships are coming right now. I want you to contact Charlie company."

Lieutenant Hollis recalls thinking he might eventually be chewed out for his less-than-formal radio language but, fortunately, foxholes are lacking not only of atheists, but also of sticklers for protocol. He never heard a word about his "shit sandwich" transmission.

Immediately, Lieutenant Hollis got on Charlie company's frequency. Charlie company, who was now about seven hundred meters away, was just now arriving at Durant's Crash Site Two. The stranded twelve-man platoon was told to hold fast. A rescue would occur very soon.

For Charlie company Commander Captain Mike Whetstone, the mission to search the Durant crash site was becoming a grim one. Arriving on the scene, Whetstone recalls the emptiness of the crashed helicopter area. An eerie roll call of names was spoken. The men from Charlie company hoped to hear at least one faint reply indicating life. A house-to-house search of the shanties surrounding the copter probably frightened a squatter or two, but no indication of what happened to the crew was given and no sign of the Special Forces rescuers turned up.

Once Charlie company was sure the area contained no Americans, the helicopter was thermolited to make sure any valuable parts still on the site would not fall into enemy hands. His first mission accomplished, Captain Whetstone had another rescue mission on his hands.

"Dragon Six, this is Tiger Six. We have found nothing at the crash site," Captain Whetstone reported to his commander Lieutenant Colonel David. "We are now proceeding to link up with elements of Alpha company in the vicinity."

"Roger."

But, as everyone knows, before linkup comes locating. The two forces had to find each other. Establishing location was accomplished by the simultaneous firing of red and green flares by both the trapped Lieutenant Hollis and the Charlie company Commander Captain Whetstone.

"Oh, shit. He's a lot farther away than I thought," Whetstone said to himself, as he saw the trapped platoon's flare sent up.

The captain and the lieutenant maintained radio communications, which allowed Whetstone to hear the vicious firefight Hollis was in. "He was very cool under fire," remembers Captain Whetstone of Lieutenant Hollis. Both men grew more anxious. They were both discovering that the straightest line between two points in Mogadishu that night was a place an American did not want to be.

Captain Whetstone knew his men could shoot their way directly to the trapped Alpha platoon, but the hail of bullets and RPGs that separated them from Alpha made that plan unwise. The APCs were the only answer even though they were not proving very invulnerable to the RPGs.

But in the midst of the battle, international diplomacy again became the most important item of business. The Malaysians could be dispatched with their armored vehicles down the road. And the issue had to be resolved in minutes, not hours.

The Malaysians who controlled the APCs, already had one of their drivers near death. They were perhaps understandably reluctant to plunge headlong into another kill zone. Simultaneous translation was not available, but the Malaysian's smattering of English allowed a discussion to occur.

"Listen, we got our wounded, but we also have two of your wounded down there. Do you understand?" Captain Whetstone asked the highest ranking Malaysian enlisted man, the one he hoped would be able to talk the other drivers into taking the trip. "It's your guys down there too."

"We get back to you," was the Malaysian's broken reply.

But after nearly an hour of further coaxing, the Malaysians still would not agree to drive their APCs to the stranded Alpha company soldiers. "We heard them talking between themselves in Malaysian," recalls Captain Whetstone. "Of course we couldn't tell what they were saying, but you could tell it was pretty passionate."

During the wait, Captain Whetstone asked Lieutenant Hollis if he thought his platoon could make a break from their entrapped positions. More helicopter gunships were called in to support them.

Within minutes, a swoop of helicopter gunships came down from the sky. "It was quite a sight as you can imagine," recalls Captain Whetstone. "You have nine helicopters in the air—without any lights. They are all firing their guns and the air is lit up with their bullets."

The sights and sounds weren't only all in the air, however. Looking down the streets, the soldiers could see burning vehicles and flaming buildings.

The minutes were ticking away with intolerable slowness. And what seemed worse to the captain was how powerless he was to rectify this situation. He ordered his men to begin fighting their way on foot to the stranded platoon.

If only his men had their own armored vehicles, the situation would be over in minutes. But Secretary of Defense Aspin had made a political decision in the previous month which the men in the field were being asked to live, and die, with. Captain Whetstone had no time to think about those things now. He simply knew that the coalition forces were not coalescing at a moment when it counted.

Captain Whetstone and Lieutenant Hollis were in continuous radio contact. Lieutenant Hollis had not been able to move from his position, but Captain Whetstone's men were having success fighting their way on foot toward the stranded soldiers. Fighting from building to building, the men approached the "kill zone." Charlie company's lead elements came to some trees and crouched down beside their captain.

A decision needed to be made. It was becoming clear that the only hope for the survival of the trapped platoon would be a charge directly through a hundred meters of hell. Without the APCs, such a charge was rapidly becoming the only opportunity for rescuing the trapped soldiers who were close to being overrun. The mission had become very dangerous.

"Listen up men," Captain Whetstone said to his soldiers. "We are going to shoot our way in. We have no other choice."

Their faces said "holy shit." Charlie company's soldiers knew they would never lack for exciting tales of combat if they ever made it out of this predicament alive.

The captain prepared for the charge. He ordered a final helicopter run to give the Somalis something to think about. And then . . . deliverance.

"I really don't know what happened, but all of a sudden, the APCs came racing up behind us," remembers Captain Whetstone. "I don't know if those Malaysian drivers did it on their own or what, but they really saved a lot of lives by coming when they did."

Sometimes in the weeks and months after the battle, the horrors and gut-wrenching fears of combat are played over and over again in a soldier's mind. They can take the form of dreams that make a soldier wake up in the middle of the night screaming in terror. Sometimes, the memories are actually pleasant. Captain Whetstone knew that what was happening as those APCs raced by with his men following would be one of those memories that he would always cherish.

Several hundred meters away, Lieutenant Hollis was not fully aware of the machinations that would bring about the rescue of his men. All he knew was that a company of APCs were now racing in his direction and that his building had been illuminated with a blue chemical light. By now, he had several severely wounded soldiers, including two who would eventually die.

Ordering his men into the open with guns blazing, Lieutenant Hollis and the remainder of his twelve-man platoon began fighting their way toward the vehicles, dragging the wounded with them. A Somalian armed with an AK-47 popped from behind a wall. He began firing his weapon from a distance of a few feet. American soldiers were wounded before a torrent of return fire cut the Somalian down.

Lieutenant Hollis tossed a smoke bomb. The men scrambled into the armored vehicles. They raced away. "Once inside, we really didn't have much to say," remembers Hollis. "A lot of the guys were bloody as hell. We were all exhausted."

The two APCs rushed in, loaded up their stranded passengers, and then made a U-turn for the return trip, linking with Captain Whetstone and his men. Quickly, Charlie company scrambled on their APCs. The entire convoy started their trip out of hell.

"Dragon Six, this is Tiger Six. Mission accomplished," Captain Whetstone reported the good news to Lieutenant Colonel David. "Second platoon secured inside our perimeter. Request further instructions."

"Tiger Six, this is Dragon Six," answered Lieutenant Colonel David. "Charlie company, you will be the first ones back. Stop at our checkpoint. Alpha company from the northern crash site will follow."

But that was one instruction that was not followed. The Malaysian drivers were not going to be stopped again. When they got back to National Boulevard they sped right through the command checkpoint. They weren't going to stop until they got to Paki Stadium.

From his window jammed with soldiers, Captain Whetstone could see what was happening. But there was nothing he could do about it. Alpha company and the lost platoon of Charlie company were back on National Boulevard racing toward the safety of Paki Stadium. Their night was over.

Chapter 12

When darkness finally came, the trapped soldiers at Cliff Wolcott's Crash Site One began to ask, "When are we going to get out of this?" It seemed they had been chased out of every alleyway and street in Mogadishu. Now they were spread out in several buildings, hunkered down simply trying to stay alive.

The men had been hearing, with some regularity, attempts by rescue forces trying to fight their way through the dangerous Mogadishu streets to get to them. None, however, had been able to get through. The men's frustration was beginning to show.

In fact, within an hour of the first crash, a hastily assembled group of Rangers led by Lieutenant Larry Moores and Sergeant Mark Warner with just four Humvees and two five-ton trucks had raced out of the airport. They followed a route that the command helicopter flying overhead believed would get them to the first crash site.

Very quickly, however, this small convoy ran into Somali small arms fire. Warner was in the lead Humvee when it turned a corner and ran straight into an ambush. Fortunately the Somalis initiated too quickly and it was not as ferocious as it might have been.

Warner quickly jammed his vehicle into reverse. He backed directly into the jeep behind him driven by Lieutenant Moores. An RPG flew right over Moores's jeep, missing his hood by inches. The men began blasting their way out of the area.

This was the kind of action Mark Warner joined the army for. If ever a man was born to be a Ranger, he was it. A slight man with an easy, fiery temper, Warner had scars on his face to show he never walked away from a fight.

He was one of those who never anguished as a young man about what he was going to do with his life. Since he was seven years old, he knew the only thing he would ever be satisfied with is the life of a soldier. His way was to be right "in the face" of anyone he dealt with. You always knew where you stood with this twenty-seven-year-old fighter. You either loved him or you hated him. There wasn't much room in between.

In fact, on this mission, when things started going wrong, Warner, who was the Ranger intelligence briefing officer, told his Special Forces commander in the TOC, "Sir, I have to go now. I'm going."

The operations commander looked Warner in the eyes and saw an intensity he knew he couldn't argue with and said, "I understand." A "no" answer wouldn't have been acceptable. Every officer in the TOC knew Warner was going regardless. "I couldn't have stayed even if I was ordered to," the young sergeant remembers.

Warner left and a "Calling All Rangers" message went out to every Ranger left on the base. Guards, staff people, cooks, and mechanics came running. The Rangers were in trouble and nothing was more important than their comrades who needed their help. Every Ranger knew that as long as there was one Ranger left to bring in, their jobs would not be done. "If you are in the 75th Ranger Regiment, it's not a job," says Warner, "it's a way of life."

After the "rag tag" Ranger convoy's first failed ambush and escape, the six vehicles led by Warner and Moores raced west hoping to find another way in. They came across a north-south road and headed north again, this time directly toward the Olympic Hotel. Almost immediately, they ran into another ambush. Their vehicles smashed against a building as the soldiers tried again to dodge bullets with only their light vehicles as protection.

"We continued our fight right there," remembers Warner. "We knew we were only a few hundred meters from the trapped Rangers but as hard as we tried, we couldn't go any farther."

Directed by Lieutenant Moores who knew that his best friend, Lieutenant Tom DiTomasso, was one of the trapped men at the crash site, the Rangers pulled back again. This time the small and battered convoy limped south. Some of the vehicles started to smoke, and others bumped along on flat tires.

They came to the K-4 circle where they hoped to swing around and try another poke into the Somali defenses. Here they ran into the battered convoy of Lieutenant Colonel Danny McKnight who was smoking his own way back from the battle. Lieutenant Moores watched one of McKnight's lead vehicles being pushed by a truck. It was apparent that the other vehicles had been shot up pretty badly.

It was clear to everyone that further rescue attempts would make no sense. Sergeant Warner, Lieutenant Moores, and the rest of the would-be rescue force reluctantly joined McKnight as their trucks and Humvees ran the final gauntlet of Somali bullets back to the airport.

Still later in the night, the trapped soldiers at the crash site heard more battle sounds in the distance. This time the 10th Mountain Division—along with Pakistani tanks, Malaysian APCs, and the Rangers—again tried to crash through Somali ambushes to get through.

The trapped Rangers at the crash site were hit by RPG rounds every five to ten minutes. There was never any significant reprieve. The fire fight never diminished as little birds made continuous strafing runs on the intersections surrounding the trapped men. The helicopters attempted to keep the Somalis down and protect the American positions.

Early in the night, most of the enemy fire was from small assault rifles but later on mortars, mines and finally 57mm rockets started to show their ugly faces. Eventually, double barreled 23mm antiaircraft guns, ZSU 23s, began firing into the American positions.

At 1:50 A.M., two and a half hours after the reinforced and armored rescue force left the airport, Captain Drew Meyerowich, the thirty-year-old Alpha company commander of the 10th Mountain Divison's Quick Reaction Force, reported to his commander, Lieutenant Colonel Bill David, that the force had finally arrived at the objective.

The trapped Ranger commander, Captain Mike Steele, knew when the 10th Mountain Alpha company was close. He warned his men not to fire their weapons unless they could verify their targets. When the lead elements of the 10th Mountain came into view through the night-vision goggles of the outer guard posts, several Rangers yelled out "Ranger. Ranger." The immediate response was "10th Mountain. Don't shoot."

Captain Mike Steele heard the exchange and came to the door of his command shack as the first elements of the 10th Mountain rescue company came down the street. "Where's your commander?" Steele asked as Captain Meyerowich appeared.

"I'm Captain Meyerowich, the commander of Alpha Two Fourteen," the 10th Mountain company commander replied. "We're here to pull you out. We brought a saw to recover the body from the helicopter. What's the situation?"

Not so willing to give up control of a situation he had been in charge of for the past ten hours, Steele made it clear he was still in charge. Pointing up the road, he gave a quick situation report, "We're scattered up this road. We have people in these buildings. The crashed helicopter is around that corner. I want you to place the APCs right there."

Having just fought for two and half hours and having suffered numerous casualties (including some KIAs), Captain Meyerowich was in no mood to discuss the nuances of operational command. He quickly notified the Ranger captain that the rescue operation was now his responsibility.

First Sergeant David Mita, the 10th Mountain Alpha company senior NCO, and a seventeen–year army veteran from Worcester, Massachusetts, felt some heat under his collar when he heard Captain Steele order his captain into position. Mita had just watched Private First Class James Martin get shot in the head. He died in his arms. Almost without thought, he interrupted the officers to address Captain Steele, "We had men die coming in here to get you, sir."

Quickly, Special Forces Lieutenant Colonel Bill Howard, who had accompanied the Quick Reaction Force, stepped forward and said to Captain Steele, "Mike, let them handle it. They are in charge." Captain Steele, the former championship Georgia Bulldog lineman, backed down. He began directing the transfer of his wounded into the APCs, pulling up alongside the Ranger positions.

Captain Meyerowich ordered a wider security perimeter around the trapped soldiers.

Meyerowich made sense. The Rangers were tired. They had been fighting for over ten hours and they were low on ammunition. The Quick Reaction Force company was fresher. They quickly established a new perimeter outside the Ranger perimeter. The extra room gave the trapped forces a rest.

Captain Steele directed Lieutenant Perino to link up with the rest of the company. Perino remembers, "I took the whooping three guys I had left and linked up with Sergeant Watson, who had been with Steele all night.

"Hey, how you doing?" Perino asked the Sergeant who slapped him on the shoulder and replied, "OK, you did good, sir."

"You did good too," Perino said. Both men realized their work was almost done.

Captain Meyerowich continued directing his three platoons to their new positions.

"I want you to establish a security perimeter from that corner to that one," he pointed as he began ordering his lieutenants. The new positions were quickly marked with infrared strobe lights so the helicopters would know where the new "good guy" perimeter was.

Incredibly, there were still civilians in some of the outer houses. The 10th Mountain soldiers tied these people up as they secured a large number of shacks. The civilians were passive and showed little resistance.

The houses were mostly 3 or 4 room shanties with no electricity. They had identifiable living rooms, kitchens, and bedrooms but very little furniture.

While Captain Meyerowich was securing the area with his 110-man force, the Special Forces lieutenant colonel moved quickly to the crashed helicopter where the body of Cliff Wolcott was still trapped in the wreckage.

The Delta soldiers who had been trapped at the crash site now came out. They began to work with their commander, Lieutenant Colonel Bill Howard, digging through the helicopter for security documents and trying desperately to free the dead pilot. The small arms fire directed at the crashed helicopter increased. One of the Special Forces soldiers was hit by a bullet and he paused just long enough to yell, "Shit." Then, almost without missing a beat, he went back to work clearing the helicopter.

"First we went through the saw blades trying to free Cliff. It was clear the blades weren't going to cut the helicopter's reinforced armor," remembers Sergeant Mark Belda, who was part of the original Search and Rescue team which fast-roped into the site almost twelve hours before. "Then we tried to pull the aircraft apart with a Humvee."

Captain Meyerowich watched as an RPG positioned directly down the street started sending rockets through the main street where the soldiers were working. He quickly ordered an APC to block the intersection. The APC gave them a few minutes of security before the vehicle was blown up.

It was now 4:30 in the morning and everyone knew darkness would soon end. Everyone was starting to get more anxious because if they couldn't get the body out soon, their biggest advantage—darkness—would soon be gone. Who could know what the Somalis had planned.

When the Humvee failed to release Wolcott from his cockpit tomb by pulling against the crushed copters, the soldiers knew there was no other choice but to wrap the pilot with a cargo strap and pull him out.

"The only thing that kept me from getting sick was that the pieces of his body didn't seem real," remembers Mark Belda with tears in his eyes. "First it was his head and arm and then it was his torso and pelvis." It was clear that the dead pilot's body was going to be taken home and no one from Task Force Ranger had any intention of leaving until the job was done. But it was a job without glory. Still Mark Belda would never be able to forget.

When the pieces of the pilot's body had been removed, Captain Meyerowich radioed his commander, Lieutenant Colonel David, and said, "Terminator Six, the body is out."

"Were all the sensitive items recovered from the aircraft?" replied David.

"That's affirmative. We're prepared to move out at this time," said Meyerowich.

By now, even the 10th Mountain was running low on ammunition. They only had one hundred rounds of Mark 19 ammo left. Meyerowich radioed all positions. He ordered that everyone remain in contact with the group immediately ahead and behind. The loading of all wounded into the vehicles was completed and within minutes, the column with over two hundred soldiers started moving out.

Sergeant Boorn, who had been wounded early in the night, had been loaded into an APC shortly after the Quick Reaction Force arrived. By now, he had been laying in the vehicle for several hours, just looking up. He remembers, "I could see the stars shining beyond the vehicle's turret. I had been looking up at the same star for about five hours now and it sure felt good to finally be moving." His APC driver was Malaysian and spoke no English, so Boorn had no idea what was going on.

The convoy started moving out.

Chapter 13

When the first truck sped back from the growing battle onto the runway at the Mogadishu Airport, Sergeant First Class John Liles, the senior medic for the 160th Aviation Regiment knew something bad was happening. The truck had its wheels shot out and it was smoking as it came crashing toward him.

Liles had seen a lot in his sixteen years of army service. But what he was about to see in the next twenty hours would go down in his personal history as his longest day, a day he could never forget.

On each of Task Force Ranger's previous seven missions, the Regiment's medical teams had set up their medical reception facilities in anticipation of something going wrong. The plan was for stabilization to occur in the triage area. Then the injured soldiers would be transferred to the army's main field hospital. On each previous mission, the medic teams were relieved that they were not much needed because nothing serious had gone wrong.

"We had our triage CCP (Casualty Collection Point) area set up and we were ready every time," remembers Liles. "Our first indication that something was going to be more than routine on this mission came when we saw that a truck come barreling in at us from the northeast. It was smoking as it came to a screeching halt right in front of me."

Other vehicles soon followed. The medics dashed to the backs of the trucks. They were shocked by what they saw. Dead bodies were stacked right on top of the wounded. "In the chaos of battle, everyone had just been thrown in there. We had our work cut out for us," remembers Liles.

These trucks were part of the first convoy led out of the battle area by Lieutenant Colonel McKnight, who had not been able to make it to Crash Site One. Already, there were over forty wounded Americans as well as several dead. The raid's prisoners were also brought in with these trucks and some were now wounded and others were dead from their hellish trip through the murderous Mogadishu streets into the airport.

Immediately, Liles started the triage process.

There were four levels of triage; immediate, delayed, minimal, and expectant. "Immediate" meant that something needed to be done right away in order to save the soldier's life. "Delayed" meant that something would need to be done soon but it could wait a few minutes. "Minimal" was something that could wait until the more important injuries were handled. "Expectant" meant that the soldier would die and no further time should be wasted.

"Things got disorganized pretty fast," remembers Liles. "Things were getting pretty ugly."

Rank had few privileges in those first few hours of chaos. There were army and air force firemen starting IVs. Full colonels were carrying supplies and comforting wounded men. There were supply sergeants and senior officers working together without thought of rank, carrying litters and placing bandages on wounded soldiers. There was even an air force veterinarian cutting off clothes and working frantically to save lives.

"We had a guy with his head caved in," remembers Liles. "We had another go into full arrest, still another soldier with a hole blasted into his leg, started to have full pulsations of arterial blood shoot from his leg. That day there were men whose hearts didn't know enough to stop beating."

The most severely injured were immediately sent to the resuscitation area where the young Dr. Bruce Adams, the 160th Regimental surgeon, and his even younger medic assistant Tommie Borton, were busily saving lives.

Coming to Somalia and getting his first taste of battle had a certain excitement for Dr. Bruce Adams. He had started his road in medicine as a student at the Armed Forces Medical School in Maryland. He then served an internship at the Walter Reed Army Hospital and had fought hard for a posting with the prestigious 160th Special Aviation Regiment.

His main competition for the job as the 160th Regimental doctor was a surgeon who was a true Ranger qualified soldier. Adams really didn't think he had a chance to become the doctor for this special unit, and he was shocked when he was selected. "I guess they figured they needed a young, aggressive doctor and they didn't care that I wasn't a full combat soldier as well," says Adams.

When it came time to leave with the regiment on August 27, Adams gave his wife and two toddler children kisses, but he couldn't tell them where he was going or how long he would be gone. "Honey, I'm going somewhere," Adams told his wife. "I may be gone a long time and I can't tell you where I'll be." Understandably, his wife wasn't understanding.

One of the first tasks the young doctor had after arriving in this strange new country was trying to save the life of a soldier from another unit who had been bitten by a shark. The Somalis like to dump animal carcasses into their harbor. The sharks of the Indian Ocean love the custom. Every American soldier was told to always stay out of the water, but on this day, one soldier didn't. He paid the price.

After fifty-six units of blood, the soldier died. Adams had the first taste of the horror he would have to face during the next few weeks. Like other soldiers sent to keep the peace and feed the hungry, the ferocity of the battle on October 3 caught him off guard.

"We were calling this whole Somali thing Groundhog Day after the Bill Murray movie where every day was the same as the day before," says Adams. "This was Groundhog Day number thirty-eight but it was clearly not going to be the same as the other days."

This "groundhog day" turned into a day of infamy. Dr. Adams and his Special Forces counterpart Dr. Bruce Marsh, the son of a former army secretary, had set up the Casualty Collection Point near the airport's tarmac. "The CCP is just a fancy aid station," explains Adams.

The first casualties came into the hospital in the morning. Three Marines were injured along with a Somalian translator who was killed in a mine explosion. There was still little else to indicate what lay in store for the medical units that day.

"By 3 P.M. we were watching the battle in the TOC (Tactical Operations Command) with the Ranger commander," says Adams. "We were notified that we had an injury within ten minutes of the time the Task Force left, but we figured it was just a fast-rope injury like a broken ankle."

When that first Humvee pulled up with injured men, there was a soldier inside screaming loudly from pain. It was clear he had a broken leg. But there was another Ranger named Blackburn in the vehicle also. He was quiet and wasn't making any noise at all. The doctors in the triage area concentrated their efforts on the yelling soldier.

It was the second soldier who had the fast-rope injury; but it wasn't a rope injury at all. It was more like a "no-rope" injury because during his insertion at the target building, he jumped out of his helicopter grasping for the rope which wasn't there and promptly dropped about forty feet into a cloud of dust and the hard slap from an unforgiving Mogadishu street. He was quiet because of severe head injuries. The doctors soon realized the severity of his injuries.

"When we got to him, we realized he had a closed head injury and was getting ready to die," remembers Adams. "He was unconscious and gurgling. We immediately cut his clothes off, suctioned his airways, and started IVs." Blackburn was going down fast.

Dr. Adams accompanied Blackburn on a helicopter to the 46th Combat Support Hospital (CSH) staffed by personnel from Fort Polk, Louisiana. The doctor figured Blackburn would be the most serious injury he would have all day. Just how wrong he was became clear when he returned to the CCP.

By now, the racing, "shot up" trucks had arrived and reports of a helicopter being shot down were coming in. According to Dr. Adams, "The shit had hit the fan."

"After sixty minutes, everybody that was still alive was probably going to make it," remembers chief medic Liles. "All of our more seriously injured soldiers were stabilized and sent to the Army hospital where they were placed on airplanes headed for Frankfurt, Germany, within twenty-four hours. The other soldiers, with less severe injuries, were treated and released directly from the triage area."

The Task Force Ranger Casualty Collection Point was efficient enough that only three soldiers died that day after arriving at the collection point.

Major John Uhorachak, an army orthopedic surgeon was one of the three doctors staffing the field hospital that day. He remembers: "If those men who died under our care that day had gone to a major hospital in the United States with nothing more going on, they may have made it. But, that's a pretty big maybe. The men who died had such severe injuries they were going to die no matter what we did."

The Rangers continued fighting. Twenty-five to thirty more wounded arrived to the CCP within the next hour. One of the most severe was twenty-year-old Private First Class Richard Kowalewski from Crucible, Pennsylvania, who wasn't breathing and had no vital signs. Dr. Adams immediately began examining the gravely injured soldier.

"Curiously, I noticed an overwhelming smell of gunpowder as I examined him," remembers Adams. "In addition to the smell, he had a missing left arm and leg. But another feature seemed peculiar. There was a piece of metal on both sides of his chest."

Dr. Adams was about to make a grim discovery he would never forget.

"Then I realized what I was looking at," continues Adams. "This obviously dead soldier had a quite live, unexploded rocket-propelled grenade embedded in his chest. The grenade had gone all the way through the right side of his chest and was just sitting there, ready to explode." The dead soldier was immediately and gently taken out onto the runway where an army bomb squad was called in.

Another soldier, Sergeant Lorenzo Ruiz from El Paso, Texas, was uncon-scious, but still barely alive when he was wheeled into the triage area. Imme-diately, a chest tube was placed into his chest to relieve the pressure on his lungs and a femoral line was placed to give him badly needed blood. Within minutes however, it was clear that the twenty-seven-year-old Ranger wasn't going to make it, but the team kept desperately trying until the end.

Later, replaying the scene in his head, Adams came up with calculations he knows will never be proven right or wrong. "Maybe if Ruiz was the only injured soldier we saw that day and if the surgeons weren't as terribly tied up as they were, he could have undergone the many hours of surgery it would have taken to save his life."

But Ruiz wasn't the only one and the surgeons were terribly tied up, so Adams and his co-workers will have to go through the rest of their lives comforted by the number of soldiers who did make it. And many of these soldiers made it thanks to the minutes, rather than hours, the combat life-sav-ing teams could devote to their care.

By now, the triage area looked like a scene out of hell. There were injured soldiers everywhere. The medics and combat lifesavers were working as fran-tically as they could have ever imagined would be possible.

The bodies of Kowalewski and Ruiz had been cleaned up and placed in a makeshift morgue just off the runway. There would be four more who would soon join them.

The air force had some reserve nurses rotating through their annual training assignments. They were spending much of their time comforting the less severely injured.

When Special Forces Master Sergeant Tim "Grizz" Martin arrived, his pelvis was largely missing and his close friend, Dr. Bruce Marsh, knew he was going to die. Nevertheless, the Special Forces doctor wasn't going to let his friend die without the fight he deserved, and despite the fact that Martin's injuries were not compatible with life, the team began frantic attempts to replace blood. Within minutes, the Green Beret was dead.

Lieutenant Colonel Danny McKnight, the Ranger Third Battalion com-mander had been wounded by a round of shrapnel which had smashed through the windshield of his Humvee during their desperate dash back to the base. Arriving at the airport, he was bleeding but not willing to spend time at such mundane activities as receiving treatment. A large group of his men were now trapped at Crash Site One and his goal was to arrange their rescue.

Before long, it became clear to Dr. Adams, if not the lieutenant colonel, that treatment would be necessary for the ground commander. Dr. Adams did some fast thinking about this "commander problem," something he had never been taught in medical school.

"I made a deal with him," remembers Adams. "He wanted to get back into the thick of things very quickly and if he couldn't, he was leaving anyway. So, I told him to let me wrap his arm and give him two bags of IV fluids. Then, I would let him go." The commander agreed, and for the next forty-five minutes, there was the unforgettable sight of the Ranger commander walking around the triage area comforting soldiers while holding his own IV high over his head.

By 6 P.M. there was a lull in the action. This lull provided an opportunity for the injured to receive more careful care, but Dr. Adams knew the calm wouldn't last. "The injured ground forces were pretty well trapped at the first crash site," remembers Adams. "We knew there were at least twenty to thirty more wounded who were pinned down and would be with us soon."

But no one thought it would take all night.

Later in the night, reports started coming in that the trapped men would soon be rescued and the wounded would be transported directly to Paki Stadium in the western portion of the city. Drs. Marsh and Adams quickly found helicopter transport along with the rest of their triage medics. They arrived at the stadium to find only two injured men there.

One was Sergeant Cornell Houston from the 10th Mountain Quick Reaction Force. He was already being worked on by Pakistani doctors. It was clear he had been shot in the chest. An occlusive dressing placed with good intentions over his chest caused a life threatening tension pneumothorax.

It was apparent this critically injured soldier had been overmedicated with pain medicines which were now decreasing his ability to breathe. The American medical rescue teams took over and removed the dressing. This helped but unfortunately not enough. Within three to four days, the Compton, California, native was dead in a German hospital.

Soon the chaos would begin again. The sun was rising and another receiving area was set up. The injured started coming in again. This time, the wounds were as much as fourteen hours old. The trapped medics had run out of IVs and wound dressings hours ago.

Chief Medic Sergeant First Class John Liles remembers, "The entry wasn't orderly. Vehicles with injured came flying in and started parking everywhere. We had no way of knowing which trucks had the most seriously wounded."

Before long, there were forty more injured soldiers needing treatment. In the morning sunshine, three more resuscitation areas were set up with a doctor and medic staffing each area.

"It was a madhouse," remembers Liles. "We had Pakistani and Malaysian soldiers getting in our way. Everyone was trying to help. Sometimes we had to ask people to leave."

This second phase of medical care lasted until noon. When it finally ended, the doctors and medics left on helicopters and returned to the airport which now looked like a battleground itself. There were battle-damaged trucks everywhere. One vehicle that had been shot up was leaking diesel fuel. It had been completely covered by sand to keep it from bursting into flames.

To the medics and doctors from the Task Force, this afternoon and night had been a dream, a bad dream they would never forget. While the injured were being treated, the reports throughout the night from the battle area made the night even more horrible.

Between fatigue and the raw terror of so many battle wounded, unforgettable scars were left: Crashed helicopters and trapped soldiers from battles being fought by trapped men, by men who were friends, and friends who were now dead that would never be forgotten.

Chapter 14

As U.S. forces came under a seemingly unlimited supply of Somali firepower during the evening of October 3, it became increasingly clear that the skill and tenacity of the men in the Forward Area Rearming and Refueling Point (FARP) would become more and more critical to not only the success of the mission but also the survival of trapped soldiers.

The initial Task Force Ranger assault and blocking group had gone into battle unprepared for a mission lasting more than a few hours. Armed only with light packs, M-16s and M-60s along with a minimal load of ammunition, the ground soldiers had little chance of prolonged survival in the slums of Mogadishu where the only gun control was how steadily a person could pull the trigger.

With crippled aircraft struggling to protect the trapped soldiers, and then limping back into the base along with exhausted pilots in quick need of fuel, food, and ammo, Staff Sergeant Michael Simpson knew that if there was any hope of ending the slaughter, he and his fellow FARP crew members would be part of the answer.

Simpson, the FARP chief armament technician remembers his evening in an almost offhand manner. "Somewhere in the evening, the airfield tower called and advised us that we were under fire. We were oblivious because we were busy preparing for what we thought might be some trouble."

In addition to the four armament technicians, the FARP was staffed by four fuel technicians and a medic.

The first aircraft in need of refueling showed up at about 4:15 P.M., forty-five minutes after the initial raid was launched. It was Barber 51 piloted by the 160th's lead pilot, Chief Warrant Officer Randy Jones.

"We need more rockets," yelled Jones above the roar of the still spinning helicopter blades as the aircraft settled onto the airport tarmac.

"What's up?" asked Simpson.

"Things are going badly," replied Jones. "We need to suppress."

Simpson had just heard that the Blackhawk piloted by Cliff Wolcott was shot down. Surviving crew members still alive faced death from the vicious and well-armed Somalians.

"That kind of sucks. I hope he's OK," thought Simpson as he and his crew began Jones's three minute "pit stop." This "pit stop" included reloading rockets, bullets and the ever dangerous "hot refueling" where a hot, running helicopter is quickly filled with highly flammable fuel in the presence of armed rockets and a myriad of other ammunition.

Hot refueling's potentially lethal combination of ammunition and highly flammable gas is dangerous. No other unit in the army would ever attempt it, let alone practice it. But the men of the 160th Special Aviation Regiment did so regularly. Only after extensive practice does the cocky attitude of the rearming crews, who do their jobs better than anyone else, develop.

"There is no real danger if you know what you are doing," says Simpson with a breezy confidence nurtured by twelve years of training. "Repetition breeds success and we knew well what we were doing that night."

The downing of the second helicopter a few minutes later left Simpson and the other FARP members with a pretty good idea that they would be working most of the night.

"Once we realized that we had a full scale battle going on, we knew we had only enough supplies for another six refueling 'iterations,' " remembers Simpson. "We called back to the TOC (Tactical Operations Center) and requested more ammunition."

The men were quickly resupplied with 7.62 ammunition, "Alpha 165," and more H-534 17-pound rockets. Throughout the night, a total of 50,000 rounds of Alpha 165 and 63 rockets were loaded onto helicopters to be rained down on the enemy soldiers. Simpson and his men knew that the battle to protect the trapped ground troops began with them.

Aircraft started coming into the FARP regularly. Pilot Chuck Harrison told the support crew during his first stop, "Things have changed a bit from the initial briefing. There are lots of rounds being fired." This wasn't really necessary as Simpson and his men began to notice bullet holes appear all over the helicopters.

The three-minute pit stops continued. "We repaired jammed guns, mechanical malfunctions, and we sometimes replaced fixed platform guns in a single minute," recalls Simpson. "We even repaired rockets and more miniguns than I can remember throughout the night."

On one of Hal Ward's early stops, he yelled for more ammo. One of the ground crew started loading one of the little bird aircraft's fixed nose guns. "No, I need M-16 ammo," Ward quickly yelled.

Simpson quickly scooped some up for him and then realized, "This pilot is shooting his machine gun out the side of his aircraft." The crew quickly found more M-16 ammo for his return.

Updates on the tense battlefield situation would regularly be provided by Randy Jones, while the other pilots just stopped long enough for the basics.

"Often the pilots would step out of the aircraft just long enough to relieve themselves and then step back into their cockpits," remembers Simpson. "We brought food out there for them and they would sit in their aircraft and jam the food down their throats." Early in the evening, a meal of macaroni and cheese was brought for the FARP crews, but these meals were quickly given to the next set of pilots rotating through.

The FARP crews and the pilots in the field knew they depended upon each other for their lives. Their interdependence was regularly acknowledged even during this tense battle situation with a regular wink or quick nod.

"We received frequent 'keep it up guys' and unsolicited 'thanks' from the pilots throughout the night," remembers Simpson. "And we gave our share of 'good job guys' back."

But Mogadishu's less-than-ideal climate was one more challenge for everyone. The nighttime temperatures of 90 degrees were starting to take their toll on the increasingly weary pilots.

The FARP crews watched as their pilots started looking more tired and sweaty. Supplying the pilots with water became more important as time went on. As dawn approached, the FARP grew quieter for any conversation would only be cause for more fatigue.

Finally, as the sun was rising after the all-night battle against the enemy and fatigue, Simpson was informed by Chief Warrant Officer Randy Jones on his final stop that, "This is it."

Not much was said as the men of the FARP began to clean up the area. "Even though we were exhausted," remembers Simpson, "we did manage a few congratulations for each other. There were more than a few pats on the back for everyone."

Chapter 15

The first light of morning was starting to show as Cliff Wolcott's body was removed from his helicopter cockpit tomb. It was 5:20 A.M. and the many wounded had long ago been loaded onto the Malaysian and Pakistani vehicles. They waited only for the convoy to begin the anticipated fight out.

Lieutenant Colonel Bill David, the commander of the 10th Mountain Quick Reaction Force, had set up his command post about a kilometer south of the crash site on National Street. He was concerned that the light of day was going to spell major problems. The Somali defenses had been preparing for this moment all night long. And they were itching to fight.

"Pick up the trail," was the order given to 10th Mountain First Sergeant David Mita as he arranged his three platoons for the trek out. "Third platoon in the lead. First to follow and Second platoon brings up the rear," was the order. It was quickly implemented. The Rangers were told to march next to the APCs and the rest would march directly behind Second platoon. Mita stayed behind with the rear guard.

"Red one up," was the command given as the convoy began to move out. "Don't break contact with the element behind and keep pace so we don't lose anyone," was the advice given by Lieutenant Colonel David to Captain Meyerowich.

"We started to move forward," remembers Mita. "As we left our perimeter, the Somali fire increased just like we expected." After the procession started, Mita watched Specialist John Seipel get hit. Seipel spun around and dropped his weapon. Not badly injured, Seipel ran across the street toward Mita, who quickly said, "Go back and get your weapon."

Protesting, the frightened young soldier told his sergeant, "But First Sergeant, I just got shot over there." Looking straight into the sergeant's face, Seipel realized his boss did not intend to discuss this matter further, so he asked, "Are you going to cover me?"

"Of course," was the reply. Specialist Seipel darted back across the street through the Somali fire, retrieved his weapon, and dived into an alley.

By now, the lead elements were starting to speed up. They were receiving direct fire from the front, but they did not intend to move slowly while they were being fired on. So they sped up. The convoy began crashing right through the Somali positions.

Unfortunately, this spearhead had the effect of spreading the convoy out. And that created a problem for the Rangers at the rear of the column who were running beside the armored personnel carriers.

The Rangers had been using the armored vehicles for cover from the intensifying Somali fire. When the column sped up, the Rangers were left behind, exposed, and running for their lives.

Ranger Specialist Melvin DeJesus remembers, "We had loaded up the wounded and were getting ready to move out. There were about forty Rangers running beside the APCs. All of a sudden, the APCs took off, leaving us with no cover. We were alone in the streets."

The Rangers bringing up the rear started running harder. They fought building to building and block to block. They were desperate to keep up with the column of rescuers now speeding away from them. The exposed soldiers later called this run for their lives the "Mogadishu Marathon."

The widening column started making lefts and quickly made contact with the 10th Mountain Command element. A whirlwind of fire started raining down on the convoy. The Malaysian drivers decided to keep moving. They left the rest of the convoy just as the Malaysian drivers transporting Charlie company had done earlier. The vehicles made a direct charge to Paki Stadium, leaving everyone else behind.

Lieutenant Colonel David was livid.

"What the hell is going on?" demanded the colonel on the radio. "I'm telling them to stop and they are not stopping," Captain Meyerowich reported.

The Pakistani and Malaysian soldiers were not bad soldiers and they had good officers. They had never been under fire before and, according to Lieutenant Colonel David, "Frankly, they had no commitment to being where they were. They had people trying to kill them and they figured they had done enough. It was time to get out of this situation and that's what they did."

The 10th Mountain Cobra helicopters overhead could see the foot soldiers being left behind. They radioed the situation in to headquarters. The commanders in the TOC could also see what was happening from their real-time videos beaming down to them from the Navy Orion spy plane flying high over Mogadishu.

The lead American elements of the convoy still had their hands full fighting pitched battles against Somali ambushes. Now, with the Malaysian as well as the Pakistani drivers out of control, it was clear that the convoy was breaking up fast.

From the TOC, Brigadier General Gile radioed to the convoy that the rear foot elements needed help. Lieutenant Colonel David ordered the part of the convoy still under control to stop. Most did. But some vehicles driven by the Malaysians kept crashing forward.

With most of the convoy stopped, Captain Meyerowich dispatched 10th Mountain soldiers to fight their way back and help the Rangers, who were still running down the street to catch up with the convoy.

"Those helicopters saved us," remembers Ranger Specialist DeJesus. "The brass casings from the bullet cartridges came down around us like rain." There were secondary explosions everywhere as the battle heated up near National Street. "I remember Mike Hawley and me promising each other that if one of us didn't make it, the other would tell the families what happened."

First Sergeant Mita wasn't having such a good time during this exit either. "One of my men got shot in the neck, and I was trapped with him behind a building." There were Somalis up an alley who knew the two men were trapped.

A 10th Mountain Cobra helicopter also could see what was happening. The Cobra began laying circles of fire into the alley. Mita noticed that every cycle of the Cobra had the Somali snipers looking up at the helicopter and ducking for cover. Mita figured this cycle would be his opportunity to escape.

"The next time the Cobra came around, we quickly darted across the street to the next alley while the Somalis were ducking." The snipers lost track of their prey, and the two soldiers connected again with elements of the convoy.

Finally back on National Street, the convoy formed again. A few hundred meters down the road, it became clear the worst was over. There were still periodic gun shots but, incredibly, women and children appeared in the streets and began chanting.

All night long, the soldiers had fired at anything that moved. All of a sudden, they went from armed conflict to a parade. People were cheering, jeering, and chanting.

"I was shocked at how well my men handled the sudden transition from a huge firefight to seeing civilians lining the streets to chant at them," says

Lieutenant Colonel David. "The emotions were still pretty intense at this time. And this civilian phenomena was giving us complete emotional confusion. I'm actually kind of surprised a bunch of civilians didn't get killed."

By 5:45 A.M., the convoy made it to the stadium. It was a pretty tense fifteen minutes while the Rangers, the Delta Force, and the 10th Mountain soldiers counted casualties. More intense moments followed as the checks proceeded to make sure everyone was accounted for, to make certain no one was left behind.

"God, there were a lot of wounded guys lying around," remembers Captain Meyerowich. "The real slap in the face occurred when I looked to my left and saw the dead bodies lying there. They weren't even covered yet."

The soldiers were exhausted. Most of the uninjured moved into the stadium seats to wait. They watched as the wounded were taken out of vehicles, treated, and then loaded into helicopters. More than a few waves were exchanged between the American soldiers.

These soldiers knew that they had looked death in the face that night. And that night they had won. They also knew that they had pushed their luck about as far as it could be pushed.

Soldiers were seen crying with each other, especially when the names of dead comrades began to be confirmed. Ranger Sergeant Mark Warner remembered a conversation he had with Sergeant Lorenzo Ruiz at a volleyball game less than twenty-four hours before about their dreams for the future, about the Thanksgiving dinner planned for next month with their families in Atlanta. Now that seemed ages ago to Sergeant Warner because his friend, Sergeant Ruiz, was dead.

Some nonattached soldiers started taking "buddy photos" with dead bodies in the background. Sergeant Warner became angry. He approached the group.

"What you are doing is very wrong, disgraceful," he said calmly. "You need to leave now. You will die if you stay."

At first one of the soldiers thought Warner was kidding. He quickly realized his mistake. It was clear there existed a danger that was very real.

The buddy photos stopped. Soon, the photographers were out of the stadium. Mark Warner watched without emotion.

When the confusion had passed, Major Nixon from the Rangers came up to First Sergeant Mita and said, "Thank you, Sergeant, for helping us." Mita responded, "No problem sir. There is nothing to be thankful for. If it were you, you would have done the same."

A little while later, the word went out that everybody was accounted for. "I was relieved we had everybody, but I felt terrible about the guys who gave their lives," Lieutenant Colonel David remembers. "I knew what had happened that night was something really big. I just didn't know how big."

It was finally over, the end of a long day and an even longer night.

Chapter 16

For some, the action of October 3–4 will never end.

Eighteen young men died for a cause their families may forever have difficulty understanding. Many other men of Task Force Ranger were wounded physically, but wounded also in that part of themselves which would never question the leaders of their own country who would apparently so readily sacrifice them.

Within three months of the raid, Secretary of State Les Aspin had resigned after some of the most intense criticism ever leveled against a Pentagon chief. Within six months, President Clinton admitted that he had not even been made aware when these men had been sent on this terrible mission with such poor back-up capability.

The father of fallen Corporal James Joyce wrote in *Newsweek* magazine, "I believe President Clinton wants the nation to forget those eighteen brave young men who died last October trying so courageously to accomplish the frivolous mission he gave them." Anger was so intense from some of the families of returning soldiers that when visited in Walter Reed Army Hospital, fathers and mothers would walk out of the room when high Pentagon officials visited.

But with the failures of the high command structure, the success of the American spirit as it existed in Task Force Ranger was incredibly clear.

These men consisting of Fort Campbell's 160th Special Aviation Regiment, Fort Drum's 10th Mountain Division, Fort Benning's 75th Rangers, and Fort Bragg's Delta Force so distinguished themselves that night of October 3 that they have become the most decorated American fighting operation in U.S. military history.

In fact, more Bronze Stars, Silver Stars, and Distinguished Service Crosses were given for actions during this evening than in any other single action of this size in U.S. military history. In addition to the Distinguished Service Crosses given to army members, a Navy Cross was given to a Delta Force SEAL and an Air Force Cross was given to an air force special forces soldier.

But, even more importantly, the first Congressional Medals of Honor in twenty-two years were given for military actions. These were given to Sergeants Gordon and Shughart who knowingly gave their lives at Crash Site Two to save the lives of fellow soldiers.

To understand how real these "unfortunate losses" were to their families, nothing can tell the story better than a letter Special Forces Master Sergeant Gary Gordon wrote to his wife Carmen Gordon. This was a letter which was found in his personal effects returned to his wife, along with his mutilated body. Carmen Gordon didn't at first even know the letter existed, which was only to be opened in the event of her husband's death.

The letter said, "Carmen my love, you are strong and you will do well in life. I love you and my children deeply. Today and tomorrow let each day grow and grow. Keep smiling and never give up, even when things get you down. So in closing my love, tonight, tuck my children in bed warmly. Tell them I love them. Then, hug them for me and give them both a kiss goodnight for daddy."

Epilogue

Within a month of the October 1993 raid, President Clinton announced that all American troops would leave Somalia by March 31, 1994. Due to this withdrawal, by February 1994 the United Nations voted to scale down their remaining operations in both numbers and authority. The peacekeeping troops no longer had the authority to disarm Somali warlords and factions by force.

The Somali warlords had clearly won the ability to continue the slaughter among themselves without outside interference.

"Somalis cannot expect assistance to continue where relief workers and logistic facilities are attacked and relief supplies are looted," said U.S. Ambassador Madeline Albright. "The United Nations will do their part to protect this humanitarian effort, but it is up to the Somalis to assure enough security for humanitarian assistance to continue."

The security was never provided and the humanitarian military forces left.

Now Somalia was back where the country started from when the Americans arrived in December 1992. There was no question that thousands of Somalis were fed during the months of American presence; Somalis who would otherwise have starved. But Somalia was left nowhere nearer to establishing the kind of political system which might prevent mass starvation in the future.

Meanwhile, the world's sole remaining superpower is still trying to figure out where its interests lie in the world; a world where the brutal atrocities splashed across our newspapers and television screens no longer present the grave threat to American security that might have been in past years.

But, then again, it was just over 130 years ago that the bloodiest day in the history of conventional warfare occurred—it was a civil war too. The Battle of Antietam occured on September 17, 1862. On this day 25,000 Americans slaughtered each other within a twenty-four-hour period. Interestingly, this battle passed with nary a call from the great world capitals to "do something about it."

Perhaps the leaders of the world of that day knew something we are only just beginning to learn now.

Glossary

Armored Personnel Carriers (APC)—German made vehicles under Malaysian command used to transport rescue troops to crash sites to protect them from RPGs.

Battle Dress Utility (BDU)—Uniforms worn for battle.

Blackhawk—Large transport helicopters two of which were shot down on October 3.

"Black Sea"—Nickname for crowded slums of Mogadishu full of Aidid supporters and hostile to the U.S. and U.N. forces.

CAR 15—Variation of fully automatic M-16 rifle.

Casualty Collection Points (CCP)—Area outside hospital where triage was first conducted on the wounded soldiers.

Combat Search and Rescue (CSAR)—Blackhawk held in reserve to aid in search for any downed aircraft.

Delta Force—Troops based in Fort Bragg, North Carolina, specially trained for high-risk operations.

Five-ton trucks—Lightly protected vehicles first used to transport rescue troops to crash sites.

Forward Area Rearming and Refueling Points (FARP)—Site at headquarters where troops got rearmed and vehicles got refueled.

Groundhog Day—Joking reference to life in Somalia where everything is same day after day like popular Bill Murray movie of that year.

Humvees—Jeep-like military vehicles.

Kevlar—Material used in bulletproofing.

K-4 Circle—Central location in Mogadishu separating warring forces.

KIAs—Troops killed in action.

Laurie—Codeword for Blackhawks to depart from air over target site after prisoners loaded.

M-48—Outmoded U.S.-made tanks under Pakistani command that aided rescue mission night of October 3.

Military Operations Urban Training Center (MOUT)—Mogadishu site where QRF Bravo company conducted urban guerrilla training.

New Port—Area near sea in Mogadishu where rescue mission was organized and launched night of October 3.

Night Vision Goggles (NVG)—Infrared goggles designed to allow troops to see at night.

"Night Stalkers"—Nickname for 160th Special Aviation Regiment.

160th Special Aviation Regiment—Secret air unit based in Fort Campbell, Kentucky, sent to transport and protect with fire power Delta and Special Forces troops on missions.

Quick Reaction Force—The 2nd Battalion, 14th Infantry Regiment of the 10th Mountain Division on alert to assist missions in need.

Rangers—Unit based in Fort Benning, Georgia, specially trained for high-risk snatch operations.

"Raven"—Nickname for 10th Mountain QRF attack helicopter company.

Rocket-propelled grenades—Deadly grenades launched by rockets left over from Soviet era abundant in Mogadishu slums.

Tactical Operations Center—Mogadishu site at airport where Task Force Ranger coordinated October 3 mission.

Target building—Building in central Mogadishu next to Olympic Hotel where top aides to Aidid were kidnapped from on October 3.

Task Force Ranger—Unit put together and coordinated by Army Rangers to conduct October 3 mission.

Index

Adams, Bruce, 82–83, 84, 85–86
Aidid, Mohammed, 1, 58, 59
Aircraft, 1, 2, 3, 4, 7, 14
Albright, Madeline, 101
Aspin, Les, 63, 99

Belda, Mark, 15, 17, 79
Belman, John, 23–24, 31, 33, 36
Blackburn, Sergeant, 11, 83–84
Blackhawk helicopters, 14
Boorn, Sergeant, 34–35, 80
Borton, Tommie, 82
Briley, Donovan, 17, 24

Carlson, Tory, 27
Carroll, Sergeant, 50–51
Casper, Colonel, 46
Casualties, 99
Cavaco, James, 27
Civilians, involvement of, 11–12, 15,
    78, 95–96
Cleveland, Bill, 9, 42, 55
Clinton, Bill, 99, 101
Combat gear, 8

Combat Research and Rescue (CSAR)
    team, 15–19, 31–37
Congressional Medals of Honor, 100
Cugno, Ron, 2, 41, 42

David, William, 45, 46, 47, 48, 51,
    61–62, 63, 64, 67, 68, 70, 73, 77,
    79, 93, 94, 95–96, 97
Decorations, 100
DeJesus, Melvin, 94, 95
Delta Force, 1, 4, 5, 8–9, 11, 41, 99–
    100
DiTomasso, Tom, 9, 22, 23, 31, 34,
    35, 36, 76
Doody, Gary, 48, 49, 50–51
Durant, Lorrie, 57, 58
Durant, Michael, 9–10, 39–40, 42,
    44, 47; capture of, 53–59

Elliott, Sergeant, 12, 34
Equipment: aircraft, 1, 2, 3, 4, 7, 14;
    lack of, 63, 72; weapons and ammu-
    nition, 5–6, 10, 15, 32, 77, 90, 91
Eversman, Sergeant, 11

Fields, Tommie, 9, 41, 55
Fillmore, Earl, 34
Flaherty, Michael, 46, 49, 50
Fort Benning's 75th Rangers, 1, 4, 7, 76, 99–100
Fort Bragg's Delta Force, 41, 99–100
Fort Campbell's 160th Special Aviation Regiment, 1–2, 5, 14, 53, 64–65, 82, 90, 99
Fort Drum's 10th Mountain Quick Reaction Force, 35, 36, 44, 45–51, 62, 64, 67–73, 77–80, 93, 99–100
Forward Area Rearming and Refueling Point (FARP), 89–91
Frank, Ray, 40, 41, 42, 55

Garrison, William, 1, 8, 46, 47
Gile, Greg, 48, 51, 95
Goffena, Michael, 5, 13, 14, 15, 16, 39, 40, 41, 43–44
Goodale, Sergeant, 37
Gordon, Carmen, 100
Gordon, Gary, 41, 42, 44, 55, 56, 59, 100
"Groundhog Day," 7, 83

Hall, Mason, 41, 42, 43
Halling, Bradley, 43
Harrison, Chuck, 90
Hawley, Mike, 95
Heard, PFC, 12
Hollis, Mark, 68–69, 70, 71, 72, 73
"Hot refueling," 90
Houston, Cornell, 86
Howard, Bill, 78, 79

Jollota, Dan, 15, 16, 17, 18, 19, 23, 31, 32
Jones, Keith, 16, 22, 23, 39, 43
Jones, Randy, 1, 2–6, 9, 41, 90, 91
Joyce, James, 100

Knight, Richard, 62

Kowalewski, Richard, 84
Kulsrud, Larry, 3, 42

Lamb, Al, 15, 16, 32, 33
Liles, John, 81–82, 84, 86–87

McKnight, Dan, 27, 28, 29, 30, 33, 76, 77, 82, 85
Maier, Karl, 16, 22, 23, 39, 42
Malaysian troops, 63, 64, 67, 71, 72, 94
Marsh, Bruce, 83, 85, 86
Martin, James, 78
Martin, Tim, 85
Matthews, Tom, 1, 18, 21, 39
Medical facilities, 81–87
Meyerowich, Drew, 69, 77, 78, 79, 80, 93, 94, 95, 96
Military Operation Urban Training (MOUT), 45
Mita, David, 78, 93–94, 95, 96
Montgomery, Major General, 49
Moores, Larry, 75, 77
Multinationals, in rescue effort, 61–80

"Night Stalkers," 2, 53
Nixon, Craig, 62, 96

160th Special Aviation Regiment, 1–2, 5, 14, 53, 64–65, 82, 90, 99
Operation mission and plan, 8–9, 13–14

Pakistani troops, 63, 64, 65, 94
Paymer, Eugene, 51
Perino, Larry, 7, 8, 9, 10, 11, 12, 21, 22, 31, 33, 34, 35, 36, 78
Personnel Locator System (PLS), 18
Powell, Bill, 27, 28, 29, 30
Powell, Colin, 63

Quick Reaction Force Alpha company, 67–73

Ranger Creed, 39
Rocket Propelled Grenade (RPG) fire, 5
Rodriguez, Specialist, 35
Ruiz, Lorenzo, 85, 96

Seipel, John, 93–94
75th Ranger Regiment, 4, 7, 76, 99–100
Shannon, Paul, 41, 43
Shughart, Randy, 41, 42, 44, 55, 56, 59, 100
Simpson, Michael, 89, 90, 91
Smith, James, 34, 35, 36
Somali: troop withdrawal from, 101; warlords, 1, 3, 100
Stebbins, Specialist, 24, 34, 36
Steele, Mike, 8, 9, 10, 11, 22, 33, 34, 35, 77, 78
Survival, Evasion, Resistance and Escape training, 53–54

Task Force Ranger Casualty Collection Point, 81–87

Task Force Ranger Tactical Operations, 1–3, 83; mission and plan, 8–9, 13–14
10th Mountain Quick Reaction Force, 35, 36, 37, 44, 45–51, 67–73, 77–80, 99–100; "Raven" attack helicopter company, 62, 64, 93
"Top ten hit list," 1, 8

Uhorachak, John, 84
U.S. Army John F. Kennedy Special Warfare Center and School, 53
U.S. Army Rangers, 1, 4, 7, 76, 99–100

Wade, Hal, 3, 4
Ward, Hal, 17–18, 40, 41, 42, 91
Warner, Mark, 75–76, 77, 96
Weapons and ammunition, 5–6, 10, 15, 32, 77, 90, 91
Whetstone, Michael, 48, 49, 51, 70, 71, 72, 73
Wolcott, Cliff, 5, 6, 13–14, 15, 17, 22, 24, 75

Yacone, Jim, 43

About the Authors

KENT DeLONG is an internal medicine physician practicing in southern California, and serves as the attending physician for the Congressional Medal of Honor Society. He is an officer in the U.S. Army Reserve, and the author of *War Heroes: True Stories of Congressional Medal of Honor Recipients* (Praeger, 1993).

STEVEN TUCKEY is the editor of a daily newspaper in southern California.